WOUNDED IN Worship

"A Preacher's Daughter Journey from

Wounds to Wholeness"

LATONYA RENAE

Edit by: Charmaine Castillo
Cover Design By: Michael L. Livingston II
ISBN: 9798218164966

DISCLAIMER

This is MY Story. I repeat ... this is MY Story. Some names have been changed to protect the blameless. It is not my desire to wound or damage those who are related or attached in any way to my violators.

Prayerfully, the negative incidents, events, and traumas associated with me will cause those who violated me to REPENT.

Forgiveness is not forgetting; it's remembering without pain

-CELIA C

CONTENTS

THANK YOU'S

God, I thank you for your love.
You are the sustainer and healer of my soul. Thanks for redeeming me.
You are my BEST friend.

To my birth father, the late Vincent Gilmore;
Thanks for being my personal angel. I miss you terribly and I hope I am making you proud! R.I.H.
See you in the morning.

To my father, William;
Thanks for CHOOSING to love me. To my mother, Altamease;
Thanks for CHOOSING to keep me.
Thanks to you both for teaching and sharing JESUS.

To my sister Kinetra, brothers Quandrell, Vincent and William; I love you.

To Kimberly, Khayree, Khamani, Darriell, Brianna, Nia, and Maxwell; I couldn't love you more if I had birthed you. Auntie loves you!!!!
To the entire Stephens, Gilmore, Jackson and Andrews families;
I am because you LOVE me.

To Mama Alinda Gadson; Thanks for saving my heart.

To Candice P. Blount;
You are the epitome of friend. Thanks for your love and protection.

To ALL my sister friends;
Thanks for giving me communion, belonging, and a soft place to fall. Thanks for seeing the best in me and seeing beyond my fallen condition. Praise Yahweh!!!

To my spiritual brothers, Alvin L. Daniels, Jr., Thomas 0. Fitzgerald, Jr., Andrew Braxter and Robert Hairston;
Thanks for always being there for me without judgement. You know me and you lovc mc anyway.

To Pastor Dr. Kevin A. Williams; Thanks for making church safe.

To my spiritual mentor, Apostle Gloria Samuels; Thanks for teaching me to be unapologetically amazing.

To Dr. Anthony Smith;
Thanks for being the best psychotherapist a lady could ask for. Thanks for being the initiator of my journey of healing.

Special thanks to Dr. Michael Dublin, Sr. for teaching me a long time ago to live and just be. Thanks for doing the foreword of my book.
Special thanks to my sis, Renee Huffman of Women of Dignity Media, and her staff for all your support and dedication to me and this project.

SPECIAL THANKS to those who sexually, physically, spiritually, mentally, and emotionally abused me. Thanks for your seed to birth and develop my ministry. Thanks for wounding me so God could be glorified! Thanks for the pain that God turned into purpose.

ULTIMATE THANKS TO JESUS FOR STAYING ON THE CROSS!!! THANKS FOR CONQUERING THE GRAVE!!! THANKS FOR RESURRECTION

FOREWORD

PASTOR MICHAEL L. DUBLIN, SR., M.A.

When I was asked to write this foreword, I was both surprised and hesitant not because of the person requesting it, but whether or not I would have the words to express what's on my mind and in my heart after knowing LaTonya for most of her life.

As a pastor who has heard her unfolding story of pain and renewal, I want to be careful to express the pain and concern I feel when a person expresses their life struggle after abuse during childhood. I can't feel what she feels, but I can clearly see the results and aftermath of her childhood trauma.

I appreciate the upward climb that LaTonya expresses throughout this book and not stopping at blame and shame, as is too often the case when great wounds have been inflicted upon a child. The hope that comes from and through her are evident as LaTonya, holding fast to her Christian beliefs, continues to not only overcome her lifelong struggle for personal healing, but by also serving as an advocate for those who have undergone similar trauma.

I have a deep appreciation for her reference to current statistics, rather than merely an emotional appeal, to make her points which shows how conscious she is of the communal effect of childhood trauma and the lack of adequate resources to meet those needs especially in the church. There is a need for advocates like LaTonya in every congregation, regardless of the size of that congregation.

I am encouraged by LaTonya speaking at conferences, lectureships, and establishing her own conference to promote changes within the church. Because of a lack of understanding of childhood abuse and trauma, the church is often in denial; but this book will deeply touch the hearts of many and cause LaTonya's story to be a driving force for change for children.

Let this story give hope for redemption and lifelong healing to those abused children and adults whose lives have been impacted in destructive ways. Read and step into this compelling story, then step out and reach out to the victims of childhood abuse and trauma for they await you - even if they don't know that.

Pastor Michael L. Dublin Sr. M.A.
South Central Church of Christ
Raleigh, NC 27610

INTRODUCTION

Does childhood trauma last forever? This has been debated over and over. Science clearly answers with a resounding YES! However, some "religious" environments say NO! Science says that childhood trauma has negative effects on the growth and development of the brain. It is very traumatic for any child not to feel loved, supported, and safe. Where trauma is present in a child, the brain lacks the ability to gain (grasp) proper attachment. Proper attachment means when a child cries, gestures, or otherwise expresses their need, an adult responds in an appropriate way. The key word is "appropriate." If a child has been handled inappropriately during the brain development process, these unhealthy practices affect the way the neutral pathways are formed. Science also says "trauma can cause lasting changes in the areas of the brain that deal with stress namely, the amygdala, hippocampus and prefrontal cortex. Childhood trauma often causes psychological issues, for example: adult ADHD, anxiety, depression, dissociation, impulsivity, low self-esteem, PTSD, high stress levels, sexual addiction, and substance abuse".

This has been the war I have been fighting all my life and to be totally transparent, I have been seeking resolution for my childhood trauma for as long as I can remember. Dr. Dharius Daniels said, "The area where you are hurt the most, will become your passion," and this has been so evident in my life. Those who know me, can attest to the fact that I am an advocate for those who have been, or who are being, abused. I have no problem being a voice for the voiceless. It comes naturally for me to stand in the gap with boldness for children, women, and men who can't find their own strength, even though, for years, it didn't dawn on me that I needed to be my own voice as well. I didn't understand that I was seeking my refuge vicariously through others finding theirs.

Childhood trauma is defined as: "The experience of an event by a child that is emotionally painful or distressful, often resulting in lasting mental and physical effects." I am the poster child for lasting mental and physical effects and I wore the badges of anxiety, depression, low self-esteem, PTSD, substance abuse, and sex addiction just to name a few.

But I am a preachers' daughter! I believe in deliverance! I am a firm believer in overcoming! I believe anything and everything can be healed; however, I don't believe that covering your pain with denial, secrets, lies and religious activity produces healing, overcoming or deliverance. Trust me, I've tried it! You must acknowledge and confront the deficits in your life, and you must be willing to get to the core of a thing to find its root.

(*where it began*). It has been my observation that the church would rather judge behavior (*symptoms/fruit/results)* instead of digging to find the source (root/core) of a thing.

Can God Heal? Can God Redeem? Can God Restore? Can you be made WHOLE? In Christ are ALL things made new? The "Religious" community answers with a resounding YES!

Does childhood trauma last forever? Sit back and take this journey with me.

MY TRUTH

"A sickness that is hidden will eventually go public"

BISHOP TD JAKES

Truth is, since I was the Tonya life MOLDED me to be and not the Tonya God CREATED me to be, I am keenly aware I shouldn't have married anyone there were too many holes in my soul. My soul was enormously infected and septic. Life's experiences have a way of breaking the true spirit of a person. My mere existence made me sick. What sickness did I suffer from you ask? The sickness of tainted lust. When you grow up believing lust and love are synonymous, you place your soul on the road of destruction. Yep that first touch at such a young age destroyed any semblance of normality for me. I believed my strength and power resided between my legs, only to find out, this "strength" was my weakness. There I was with three failed marriages. My sickness bled out on them and everyone I came into contact with. What I used to hide, I wore as a badge displayed for the whole world to see. If only I could turn back the hands of time. If only I knew God loved me in spite of my secret. If only ...

I used to think God sanctioning me to be born was a big mistake. "I AM A MISTAKE" are the words that echoed between my ears for decades. Does God make mistakes? Can He be wrong this time? From the beginning, I was rejected. As an embryo, I heard, "You ain't bringing no baby in here!" Words uttered by the very grandmother that rescued my mother from rejection, was now rejecting me. From that moment in the womb, just like Jacob did, I began to "wrestle with God " Studies show, children born from stressed wombs are born to struggle. Have you ever felt you were born just to die? I've always been in a war just to breathe!! Did God not breathe into my nostrils so I could be a "living" soul? Why can't I breathe?

As I grew, I couldn't understand why I kept getting buried alive; especially in the place designed to give life THE CHURCH. Life for me in church was such a suffocating experience. I held my breath for decades. Do you know what happens when you hold your breath too long? Your oxygen levels go down, your brain becomes hypoxic, you feel confused, it alters your decision making, and you have a loss of coordination. Because of all the strangulation of pastors and church leaders I endured, this makes sense. I was sooooo afraid! Instead of them being ministers, they were monsters. I was confused because they were proclaiming a Jesus they didn't believe in. God certainly didn't have the power to cleanse them so how could He save me? Their spirits were contaminated by their own wounds, and they had the audacity to preach wholeness from their foundation of brokenness. Ultimately, they transferred their pain onto me. It was that dangerous venom that poisoned my soul. I bled profusely from the inside wounds that were extremely diseased. It seemed I had no hope to heal and, for me, there was no "balm in Gilead."

BUT GOD!!! It was the struggle of wrestling with God from the womb that was actually strengthening me. In each fight, He was giving me more of himself. On this journey from "wounds to wholeness," I have had to wrestle with God many times. I have had to say, '1 WILL NOT LET GO UNTIL YOU BLESS ME," and even though I may have a limp from my journey, I am eternally grateful that God never took His hands off of me. I BREATHE!!! AHHH!

Save me,0 God! God rescue me! Deliver me, 0 God! Psalm 69: 1

PRELUDE

"God bless the child that's got her own"

A FETUS BORN THROUGH TURMOIL

Her name is Altamease C. Ray. She graced earth on February 7, 1953 in Jacksonville, Florida. She is the oldest of four girls born to Gwendolyn Ray and to a man she would never see, meet, or even know his name. Sadly, she was a fatherless and motherless child whose mother abandoned her and her three sisters in a tiny apartment with only carrots in the refrigerator. As the oldest, she tried to take care of her sisters as best she could, but to complicate things, her baby sister had to have a special formula. Thankfully, she knew how to make the formula and fed her sister. Eventually, a neighbor noticed that their mother had been gone for days and was going to call social services, but instead called their maternal grandmother, Ozeal Ray. Their grandmother took guardianship of them and well actually, the girls went from "dysfunction" to a "greater dysfunction" witnessing toxicity on so many levels.

As the oldest, Altamease learned how to cook, sew, clean, and mastered the skills to successfully run a home. As destiny would have it, as a teenager, she meets a handsome young man Vincent Gilmore. They really liked each other both of them full of life and destiny then she received the news ... she was pregnant. Oh no!!!! She is only 15! Her younger sisters gave her skills to be a mother, but would that be sufficient to bring a child into the world? There were options, but instead of choosing abortion or even adoption, she wanted this child.

When her grandmother found out she was with child, she told her, "You have to get out of here. You ain't bringing no baby in this house." One of her aunts begged her not to put her out. "Mama, you're just angry," she said, but the pleas of her aunt fell upon deaf ears.

She packed her other dress and some underwear, put them in a paper bag and walked away, and as she walked, she prayed, "God, please make it so I would NEVER EVER have to go back there."

August 1, 1969, at 16 years of age, she gave birth to a baby girl, LaTonya Renae Gilmore. She would later say this child saved her life, and said to her, "LaTonya, you light up my life."

Oh yeah God did answer her prayer because she never had to go back to live with her family ever again.

CHAPTER 1

Born to Die

August 1, 1969 at 12:58 a.m., I made my earthly appearance at St. Vincent' s Hospital in Jacksonville, Florida. I was my mother's precious gift from God. I belonged to her. She said she looked at me and said, "I have my very own living baby doll." She not only loved me, but for the first time, she had someone to love her back unconditionally.

Holding me felt like her heart was beating for the very first time.

I was born 6 pounds and 6 ounces with a head full of hair, ten fingers and ten toes, breathing on my own, and healthy. The doctor and nurses congratulated my mother and said, "She's perfect."

Funny with all their expertise, no one recognized that in the short time of my existence, I had already been in a fight. As embryos, we feel what our mothers experience. Yes, I came out with the appearance of perfection, but my mother and I had already lost several battles. I wondered if they even recognized the strength it took for my mother to say yes to my heartbeats, especially after being encouraged to give me up. Can you imagine her trying to decide what would be best for me? She was never mothered, and she didn't have the support of her family. Yet, in spite of her being a single teenage mother facing unknown odds, she CHOSE me.

It's crazy, but I swear I can remember my mother's prayer to God pleading with Him not to ever have to go back to the family that rejected

US. She named me LaTonya Renae Gilmore (she didn't want me to carry her family's name).

God is so FAITHFUL! He hears and He provides. At her young age, she knew of the providence of God and in spite of our means or the lack of it, He provided us with a loving place to stay. We were welcomed into the home of my father Vincent's godmother, Wilhelmina Ross, who was very kind to us. She loved my mom and I as if we were her own. This love was special because it came without judgement or condemnation. Outside of my mother choosing to keep me, Ms. Ross was the epitome of what God's grace felt like. I also had my birth father and his family - the Gilmores and there are no hearts bigger than theirs. I had my grandmother Lavinia, Auntie Arvia, Auntie Denise (Neccie), Uncle Blaine, Cousin Renae (I'm named after her) and Cousin Denise. I was everyone's little angel pure, beautiful, wanted, and loved. We never went without and I was drenched, emerged, and covered in love.

When God listens to our prayers, He not only hears the ones we verbalize, but He also hears the ones our hearts speak. Even though I was loved, my mom yearned for a special love of her own, and boy did God answer! We were introduced to this debonair young man from the eastside of Jacksonville. I'm sure people wondered "can anything good come from the Eastside?" The answer was YES!!!! God gave us William Stephens and provided us a double portion of His love. He claimed me as his very own because my mother made it very dear we were a package deal. Our love grew and he married my mother on August 21, 1970. Oh happy day when I knew my bonus dad was here to stay. My mom was radiant. The dress she wore was tailored to her snapback figure perfectly. My bonus dad was cleaner than the board of health, and of course, I was cute in a beautiful dress with my ponytail garnished with ribbons. The cake was very decorative and Ms. Ross, the preacher and two witnesses gathered to make us one. They stood before God at 20 and 17 years of age and made a commitment for life. In addition to him pledging his undying love to her, he promised me "forever" too. Only one thing went wrong, I cried throughout the entire ceremony. No one could get me to stop crying and I only stopped making a fuss when my bonus father picked me up. I guess I just needed his attention or I had to make sure he was serious about making this deal. Of course by this time, I was spoiled rotten.

How blessed can one child be? I was the apple of everyone's eye and love was so abundant. I went from chosen to rejection to chosen again. God gave my mother and me a new start. My mother's faith increased because God's blessings and favor was so evident in our lives.

Well, me being the center of attention didn't last. Kinetra Y. Stephens was welcomed into our lives on August 11, 1971. Now I have my very own living baby doll. Her round cheeks and beautiful skin made her so precious. I had my first best friend and my heart had someone else to love and cherish.

In 1971, we also began attending Westside Church of Christ at the invitation of my birth father, Vincent. My parents got baptized and we were faithful. It was wonderful not only were we a physical family but a spiritual one as well. The decision was made we would all grow together.

On June 9, 1973, God said yes to our family once again. He said NO a year earlier we lost a baby; however our pain was replaced with joy. Quandrell A. Stephens was given to us, but he didn't come easily he came before his 9 months was up. Premature and weighing in at 3 pounds and 1 ounce, he had to fight to breathe and live. I was almost 4 years old at the time and understood the seriousness of him having to go into the NICU. I vividly remember sitting in the lobby with Sister Israel anxiously awaiting to meet my little brother.

When my brother was allowed to come home, we rejoiced. He was so small, but he was getting stronger every day. Again, God had answered our prayers. Our rejected family of two is now five strong. William, Altamease, Kinetra and Quandrell Stephens and LaTonya Gilmore. Although I had a different name, I didn't experience a different love. Besides, God was about to add to me again. My birth father, Vincent, married Diane on September 29, 1973 and it was a beautiful occasion. Not only was I in the wedding, but so was my mother and bonus dad. Yes you read that correctly all of us were in the wedding. Don't tell me everyone has to deal with baby mama drama and deadbeat dad issues we destroyed that myth. Then on June 29, 1977, I became a big sister again as my heart welcomed Vincent IL My life was full and abundant. God had given me so many people to love and to be loved by.

As time moved on, my bonus dad was so faithful to the church and began working in different ministries. He was a natural born leader and had committed his heart to us and to the work of the church. He wanted to be the best provider for his family, leader of the church and a Christian God desires. God had gifted him tremendously and it was dear, my dad declared and decreed, "as for me and my house, we will serve the Lord". In his bold declaration, he intended that his children would grow in the admonition of the Lord.

Truth is, even with the best intentions, sometimes you are the ball that gets dropped. I'm reminded of the story of Mephibosheth in the second book of Samuel. When he was five years old, there was a nurse responsible for taking care of him. In her haste to cover him and take him to a place of safety once she was informed that Mephibosheth' s father, Jonathan, and his grandfather, King Saul, was killed in battle, she picked him up, started to run with him, and dropped him. She dropped him so hard he became lame in both feet, crippling him for life.

In my life, with no bad intentions of my father, as he was on the battlefield to save souls, he left me in the hands of "church people" and I was dropped. Crippled in my heart crippled in my feet.

Have you ever tried to walk without feet? You stumble, you crawl, and sometimes you fall flat on your face. Often when one falls, especially on their face, it could cause serious injury. The crazy thing about falling is, oftentimes you don't realize at first how injured you are. Your adrenaline kicks in and it suppresses the pain. Your body experiences what scientists call the "fight or flight" hormone. Your body immediately goes into a defensive mode. It masks the injury and it's not until the adrenaline wears off that your body communicates to you something is wrong.

My personal belief is we are born pure. We are endowed with the gift of the Holy Spirit. We are born full of purpose and destiny. However, being placed in a fallen world, circumstances (things out of your control) and situations (things you create yourself), have a way of chipping away at your spirit. Before you know it, you're wounded and broken and feel

CHAPTER 2

"Why Did He Have to Touch Me"?

The day came when Ms. Ross passed away and that was my first experience with death. I didn't understand why she had to go to heaven; I wanted her to be with me. At the funeral, people were crying and saying she would be missed, yet they kept saying to rejoice because we would see her again. She laid in that box with her eyes closed, as if she was sleeping. I was thinking, "Let's just wake her up and all this crying can stop." To say I was confused is an understatement. Why did she leave me? In my spirit, I knew life would never be the same she was our safe place. They told me I could feel her presence if I kept her in my heart, so I smiled through my tears, knowing if I closed my eyes, I could always keep her alive.

With the exception of the death of Ms. Ross, up until I was about six years old, I can't remember a time when I was not smiling my life was full of joy. I had a village whose love for me was impeccable. I was a two-time big sister and I took that role seriously. I was determined to be what Ms. Ross was to me EVERYTHING.

In addition to my immediate family, there were other people who were a part of my village; and to this day in hindsight, the name given for these people makes my heart ache and my stomach upset. I now have these people called the "family of God." The love of these people was supposed to be an asset to all the other love I was receiving. In my little mind, this was going to be great. These people are those following God;

and since God was the man in heaven taking care of Ms. Ross, and He is good, I figured so were they. I don't remember the circumstances of why we didn't go to a family member while my parents had to go out of town and "preach the Gospel", but this particular night would change my life FOREVER!!

I remember watching TV, having dinner, and getting a bath. My sister and I were adorned in our pajamas in anticipation of our parents returning shortly to take us home, but as it was getting later, we were then told our parents would come get us in the morning. I remember sharing a bed with my sister in the guest room and before I drifted off to sleep, I made sure my sister was safe and sound. I fell asleep expecting the next touch to be that of my parents, but, to my dismay, it would be a touch of a "monster" I would feel.

As I slept, a hand covered my mouth. I opened my eyes and there he stood over me telling me not to make a sound. I looked over at my sister and she was sleeping soundly. He sat me up and started rubbing my shoulders then my hair then my lips. At six years old, I didn't know what to feel, but I knew what I was feeling couldn't be good. The next thing I knew, my little six year old lips were pressed against his penis. He said, "Relax and open up." I immediately prayed that my parents would come now. I looked at my sister and tears came into my eyes. He demanded that I "open up," and again, following his instructions, I tried to keep my little lips around him. When he became frustrated because I wasn't going deep enough, he grabbed the back of my head and pushed it in thrust after thrust. Next thing I knew this "liquid" was running out of the sides of my mouth and I started crying more because now my throat was sore. He put his hand over my mouth and said, "You better not tell anyone; if you do, I can make sure your daddy loses his job. No one will believe you anyway and you will get in trouble." He took me to a bathroom, wiped my mouth, put me back in the bed, said "goodnight" and walked out. I looked over at my sister and she was still resting. That was the night I died, but I didn't go to heaven like Ms. Ross. There wasn't anyone crying and saying "Amen." I am not breathing. Where is my coffin? I don't want to be here anymore. Why is my heart beating so fast? I want to go to heaven with Ms. Ross. I cried myself to sleep. The next touch would be my parents waking us up. I couldn't say a word. This church and family of God thing was working out for my dad and I can't disappoint him so I kept silent.

Just like that, my abundant love would be replaced with the death of my spirit. I was not the same child. The sad thing is, I would have to die over and over again as that night was constantly repeated. The church needed my daddy; therefore we ended up going there more times than I could count. After a while, I became used to it. As long as it was me, and not my sister, I concluded I would be fine.

Thankfully, my parents took us to other members of this family of God. In this next family, I really admired one of the sisters and I was excited to be there. She was tall, beautiful, and confident and I wanted to be her. I thought it would be amazing to be around her. However, being around her meant I would have to come face to face with another monster.

By this time, I was a pro at this molestation thing it was so routine. While everyone was having dinner and hanging out, the monster was staring at me and finding ways to bump into me. The monster gave me compliments and I smiled knowing good and well I would be in hell when everyone went to sleep. It is sad, but by the time I was eight years old, "hell" was normal. Each night he entered, I just laid there waiting for the sun to rise. I definitely wasn't going to tell a soul that would mess up everything.

I didn't understand, but I swear all the monsters in this family of God, were a part of their own community. They were not ashamed, but actually bragged to each other about their conquests. They exchanged information amongst themselves, and I know it's crazy, but a part of me was enjoying the attention. They would tell me I was beautiful and would say, "Tonya, when you grow up, you're going to have any man you desire." I would just smile, not realizing these encounters were putting more holes in my soul.

By the time I was ten, I was exhausted. These monsters were everywhere and now one was in my very own home. My parents opened our home to those in need I guess that was the Christian thing to do, but it was a cross for me. My parents were taking this family of God literally. Well, as fate would have it, this navy soldier from the church would need room and board. To this day, I don't understand that. I knew Uncle Sam normally took care of his own, so why was he there? I knew him very well because my Mom was the choral director and he was in the group. I guess you can say they were our extended family. It wasn't strange at this point that our house would be filled with "family." It was never just the five Stephens members there were always some extras. I understood my parent's heart, because when we were on hard times, others opened their homes to us, so it was only right for them to lend a hand when they could, but I often wondered why they couldn't weed out the monsters.

I have always loved the arts and was fascinated by them. It was my dream to be a Broadway star. I loved acting, music, dance, comedy you name it. There was this show back in the early 80s called "Fridays." I looked forward to Friday night because I was able to stay up later than usual. "Fridays" was a late comedy sketch series and it was my late night treat until I became the late night "trick".

Each Friday I came out and lay on the couch to watch the show. He (the monster) would be there on the other end watching the show as well. One of those Friday nights he pretended to have fallen asleep. After the show ended and I was about to exit, he pulled my arm and laid me on top of him. In my head I was saying, "no not this again," but my body cooperated to its normality. Each and every Friday, I would have this date with the monster.

I remember the day as if it was yesterday when I decided enough was enough. My poor ten-year-old body just couldn't take another moment of violation. The smile my face normally wore was gone my spirit was bound my soul was empty. That day I chose to be bold. I had to tell what Uncle Sam's and God's soldier was doing to me.

At the laundromat in the Arlington area where we lived, as I was helping fold the clothes, I was asked, "What's wrong? You don't seem like your normal self." I swallowed hard and said, "He touches me every Friday. He gets on top of me and grinds me so hard. He kisses me as though I am a woman. He doesn't make me "drink" like the others, but I just can't take it no more." I was waiting for a response of shock and anger, but instead I was met with a look of disappointment and disapproval. I knew immediately that I should have kept this secret too. I was astonished that I had to bear the weight of another adult weakness.

When I returned home, he was confronted, but instead of him being held accountable, he was allowed to call me selfish and jealous. He said, "the only reason you told, was to ruin my friendship with your mother." I stood there looking for someone to rescue me, but no one did. I died again that day. I learned that I was on my own. This family of God bond was strong, and I learned to keep my mouth shut. There was no protection from those monsters I mean, men of God. The message that stood out to me was my feelings didn't matter and a child definitely needs to stay in their place. I was numb. When I was between the ages of 10 and 13, I don't think I even blinked or cried if I was inappropriately touched this violation had become the norm.

When I was 13, my dad informed the family that we were moving far away. We were leaving Jacksonville, Florida to go to this unknown place called Durham, North Carolina. I was in conflict glad we were leaving this family of God, but I didn't want to leave my friends. I had an attitude and was angry because no one had even asked me if I wanted to move. As a child, you don't get to have a vote. I was used to the chaos. Who wants to pack up and go to a place they never heard of; and plus, I had no desire to go meet another one of these groups called the family of God. I pleaded with my parents to let me stay and live with my great grandparents, Clara, and James Stephens, but the answer was NO! Then I asked if I could stay with brother and sister Jackson because these people were God on earth. They were the only people in this family of God I felt was trustworthy. Still a resounding NO!!! I was enraged!!! I didn't want to move; however, the bright side was I was no longer going to be around the monsters so I thought.

We made the drive from Florida to North Carolina to our new home and I loved the new house. I thought I was safe; however, I didn't know my father had invited one of the men from Jacksonville to live in our home. He was there to help establish the new church in Durham. There was a lot of door knocking and outreach for the newly planted Southside Church of Christ. I remember complaining about leaving my friends and the big pretty building with a balcony to come to a little cold room. There were holes in the ceiling, cracks in the wooden floor and there was no heat. It was colder inside than it was outside. We are worshipping around kerosene heaters with our coats and gloves on. What in the world had my father said yes to? God, are you in Durham?

At church I kept hearing about this God that was supposed to love me. I couldn't figure out what I did to offend Him, but He wasn't showing up for me. To add insult to injury, He seemed to love the monsters dearly. They would be a part of the group that would come up periodically to help with the outreach of the new congregation. They continued to praise and worship in spite of their transgressions. I just didn't understand. I could no longer sing "Jesus Loves Me". Evidently, He hated me. Why did I have to be a part of this family of God? I hated it as much as God hated me. I would ask God, "Why do you, let me go through this? Why allow me to be chosen just to be destroyed? Is there a way I can get out of being me?"

Have you ever wanted to return to your mother's womb? Yes, you guessed it! The man that came with us to help build the church was another monster. He could preach and he could sing, but he was no man of God. Same access, same entry, same speech, different monster. God, why can't I escape these church monsters? What do they want from me? Better yet, God, what do YOU want from me? These are your men. Why can't you make it stop? I asked the Lord this daily. For a while, I thought God ignored me, but one day I came home from school, and he was gone. This was a victory for me. That day proved to me God did hear a sinner's prayer. The monster was gone!!!!

That victory was short lived because soon after that, another monster would be in our home. This time, I fought like hell! At 14, I had ENOUGH!!!! That particular night would not end like the rest. As I fought off the offender, my dad heard the commotion and burst into the room like superman! I swear I saw a cape and a big S on his chest. He turned on the light and pulled that monster off of me. The next day he was GONE!!!!

Finally, I could sleep through the night. NO FEAR! No one to harm me.

CHAPTER 3

"If These Church Walls Could Talk"

Try to imagine, if you will, the mindset of an abused child dealing with the dichotomy of good and evil. The church is where I learned how to praise and simultaneously lie. I felt crazy watching those who were abusing me praise God. It became my normality to say amen when my abusers partook in worship. Clearly, I became a participator in my own suffering. It felt weird to betray myself, but what other option did I have? I would sit there and ask how God could receive their offering. I couldn't understand how God's love could be so contaminated. As a child, I used to think if God is omnipresent, omnipotent, and omniscient, why didn't He send down fire to stop this church madness? I know God isn't blind He has to see that this community He named ecclesia (church), has lost direction. Somebody isn't reading the instructions His rules have gotten lost in translation.

Can you picture my confusion when I was convinced heaven and hell must be the same place? What was also unbearable was the fact that these men were men who served with my father. These were his brothers in Christ, but they were my monsters. How can Christ be the savior of the world yet He couldn't save me? Why did I have to be the sacrificial lamb on their altar of perversion? Why did my blood have to be shed?

Sexual abuse in church didn't begin and end with me. It has been an unspoken stench in the air for generations. The aroma is foul, but no one seems to smell it, and it boggles my mind how the church community has conveniently become accustomed to it. We fall in love with the gift of a person and could care less about their character. Instead of the congregation being moved by the way a preacher matriculates the rising and falling of his voice, I wish they would be angered by the abuse he administers with the rise in his pants. The church is meticulous about people coming in and getting their souls saved; however, they won't require their leaders to be holy and blameless. Why does the church subscribe to the "eyes wide shut" mentality? How could they continue to ignore the stains from the trail of blood flooding from my soul? I couldn't understand how the church was trying to convince me that I needed them to make it to heaven, but in the same breath, cultivate hell as the path to get there. A child should be able to come to the house of God and be safe. Church is supposed to be a community of God's chosen people. It's the place where His standards and values should be demonstrated. Yet, the devil ran rampant through the walls, leaving his devastation and destruction on each pillar. How can I sing while living in a strange land? What do you do when the hallelujah in your soul is haunted? For me, church symbolized death there was no life and no hope, and to me, Christ died in vain.

The sad thing is, no one came to my rescue. Instead, I was called fast and grown. I constantly heard adults saying things like, "Look at her she is always in some man's face." How can I be on trial when I didn't commit the crime? Why was I being revictimized? My soul cried because the walls couldn't bear witness to my agony. They saw things but couldn't speak. How many times have they seen a man's hands in places they shouldn't have been? How many times was a holy kiss replaced by the kiss of death? Why didn't the men get reprimanded? How can they get away with preying on a child? Why am I being punished? Why did my innocence have to be murdered? Maybe I could have lived if the walls had tongues to testify on my behalf.

God are you there? There were certain things I couldn't understand. If God could rescue Daniel in the lion's den, save the three Hebrew boys from burning in the fiery furnace and part the Red Sea so Moses could lead the Israelites out of Pharoah's bondage, why couldn't He rescue me out of the hands of these nasty men? Why won't He save me? I cried "Eli Eli Lama Sabachthani" MY GOD MY GOD, WHY HAS THOU FORSAKEN ME?

At the age of 14, instead of being guarded and swearing men off for a lifetime, I became interested in a young man four years my senior. He was a senior in high school, and I was a freshman. I felt like Celie when she spoke about Shug "He was like honey, and I was like a bee." I couldn't stay away from him. He treated me kindly and was very gentle with me. We became very close. Look at me I have a boyfriend I have protection. I could talk to him about anything, and his friends became my friends. Then it dawned on me this family felt much better than the family of God. I loved this family. I skipped school and stayed out late just to be surrounded by them and we hung out on the street corner talking for hours.

I found myself laughing and having fun. Life felt good. My boyfriend wasn't forcing anything, but I wanted to give him all of me. I decided, if I wanted to keep him, I needed to sleep with him that all the kissing and grinding wasn't going to keep him faithful, so I needed to step up my game. He was a good guy, but I knew even nice guys desired more, so we planned the night I would become a woman. Everything was going great until he tried to penetrate. I wanted it, but I couldn't. I freaked out I was embarrassed I failed him. However, he didn't walk away and remained my boyfriend until I went to college. We knew, with the distance, it would be hard to maintain our relationship, so we decided to just be friends and I was blessed to have him as my confidant for many years afterwards.

In the fall 1987, I left Durham, North Carolina for Terrell, Texas to attend the great Southwestern Christian College. I received a vocal scholarship and thank God I did, because I didn't otherwise have a plan. I was a gifted and talented honor student, but I had no real desire to be anything I was so lost. I had stopped dreaming a long time ago, but I knew I had to do something. This would be my first time on a plane and away from my family, and even though I was terrified, I looked forward to my future. I viewed it as a metaphor of baptism. My past would be washed away, and ALL things would become new. I needed this new start 8 (a new beginning) and 7 (perfection). Yes, this would be my perfect new beginning. Tears flowed as I waved goodbye to my family and friends. I would miss them, but I desperately needed to breathe. There were so many secrets I needed to erase, so many dreams deferred, and so many monsters

I wanted to die. I needed this new journey and I needed those tears of goodbye to cleanse me.

I was blessed to have some people I already knew in Dallas who met me at the airport. I arrived on a Sunday morning and as soon as I left the baggage claim, we headed to church. As I sat there, I wondered if there were any monsters in that church. I hoped not, but if there were, they better not try me. I was older now and would not be taken advantage of.

After getting a bite to eat, I was dropped off at my dorm and was so thankful for their hospitality. As I watched others taking their suitcases and boxes to their rooms, I couldn't help but notice that everyone seemed so friendly and excited to start the journey to higher education.

I must admit that my transition was smooth because my father had a close friend on staff. He had made a promise to my father to take good care of me and assured him that I wouldn't want for anything. My roommate and I got along well and since I was on a vocal scholarship, I couldn't wait to meet my music teacher. I was so excited and the first time we had choir, I was amazed by the talent in the room. I was assigned the voice part of alto more specifically, second alto, and I prayed that I would be able to stand up to the expectation of my scholarship. My section leader was fond of me and told me about the tryouts for the freshman ensemble. I tried out and I made it. I made friends easily and all was well in my world.

My daddy's friend kept his word. If I was hungry, he made sure I was fed. If I needed anything, all I had to do was ask. I could come to his office at any time and he would make sure I was taken care of.

My freshman year was good and I learned a lot. My favorite course was Old Testament Survey. This is where I began to really become acquainted with the God I should have met at church. I was excelling in my studies and having a ball traveling with the choir I even had a boyfriend who was a preacher. OMG really, Tonya? I told myself I would NEVER be interested in or marry a preacher, but he was different in that he truly lived the life he preached about. He was so sweet and was really shy until he got behind the pulpit. He was good! He was also a singer, therefore we traveled together on behalf of the school.

In the spring, there are tryouts for Summer Tour which was comprised of a special ensemble that traveled in the summer to raise monies for the school. I tried out and I made it. The only thing that was hard about ending my freshman year was saying goodbye to my boyfriend for the summer and my friends in the graduating class.

Not only was it an honor to be selected for Summer Tour, but I also lucked out because my father's friend would be the one taking us on the road. We would be under his care and because he had already taken such good care of me, I knew I would be okay. When we traveled night after night and church to church, each group of roommates would rotate between staying in the homes of some of the congregants or staying in a hotel.

I was grateful for those who opened their homes to us, but not everyone was as clean as I was. You'd be surprised how some of the saints lived. I wish I could have told them that "cleanliness is next to godliness" was in the Bible, but it turns out it was merely an old proverb in Babylonian and Hebrew religious tracts.

Finally, it was our turn to stay in the hotel. My roommates and my father's friend decided to watch a movie in our room and we all ate and talked about the tour thus far. My roommates both fell asleep and after the movie was over, my father's friend said he was about to go to bed, and as he was leaving he turned to me and asked to talk to me in the hallway. I didn't think anything of it since we chit chatted all the time about school and family. When we stepped into the hallway, he started talking about all the things he had done for me and how much he had cared for me. He reminded me of the promise he made to my dad to take care of me and asked if he had kept his promise. Of course, I said "yes" and told him I appreciated everything he had done for me and then things got weird as he tried to kiss me. Immediately I thought, "Not this mess again." I moved away from him saying, "This is wrong! I can't do this! You are my father's friend!" I told him that I had become close to his family especially his daughter, but he took the posture that I "owed him". He tried to kiss me again and forced me against the wall. I just couldn't do it I refused him and went into my room.

The next day as we were loading up the van, I said "good morning." He ignored me and I was perplexed and hurt at his display of anger toward me. We continued on to the church to meet the rest of the group who had stayed in the homes and later that morning, when I tried to have a conversation with him, he said, "I know you aren't trying to talk to me. I have nothing to say to you." I was DEVASTATED and began to cry. My friends noticed my tears but I couldn't tell them what was wrong. The silence between us lasted for days. He would not give me the time of day and I just couldn't take it anymore, so one night, at one of our concerts, I took extreme measures to get his attention I faked a whole passing out scene on stage. We were in the middle of the second half of the concert when I closed my eyes and fell backwards. I knew one of the guys on the back row would catch me so the young man that caught me carried me out and laid me down on a couch in one of the offices. They brought me something to drink and put a wet cloth on my head to cool me off. When I started blinking as if I was coming to, they asked me a few questions and then he walked in. I knew he had to come see about me, after all, he was my guardian. He asked me if I was okay, I said yes and told him I was sorry. In my mind, I was rejoicing because he was responding to me.

After the concert I was supposed to go with my roommates to the home we would be staying at for the night, but he told everyone he would bring me later. He told them he had to get me something to eat and make sure I was okay. After getting into the vehicle, I confessed that I had to do something to get him to talk to me again. We went through a Popeyes drive thru to get dinner, but before he returned me to the house I was to stay at for the evening, he said he had to stop by the hotel first. Oh how convenient, but I was just so thankful we were speaking again. After entering into his room, I took a seat in a chair while he started talking to me and clearing things from his bed.

Oh yeah, I forgot to share with you that he knew all about my life. I had told him everything, so he knew I had never been penetrated by anyone's penis. I had shared with him something that I had not shared with anyone else I was still a virgin. He knew about all the molestation and my emotional struggles, especially when it came to church leaders. He knew I didn't like being a preacher's daughter and he knew that even though my father and I loved each other, I was angry because I believed the church got the best of him and I didn't. I had shared with him how I felt like a fatherless daughter even though my dad and I shared the same address, and he knew I was jealous of all the people who received my dad's attention when I felt I should have been the one receiving all of his attention. Now looking back on it, I was easy prey He had groomed me perfectly. He knew I had felt worthless all my life and he made sure he always came to my rescue when I needed him. It's crazy but, in that moment, I felt I owed him. I didn't want him to be mad at me, so I decided I had to pay up.

As my body ached between my legs, I felt my soul and spirit leave. Those familiar tears came streaming down my face because I knew the blood indicated "I am wounded". I cried out because the pain was excruciating. He just whispered, "Relax I got you." I closed my eyes and had an out of body experience I was watching him wreck my body. This place was so familiar. When he was done, I opened my eyes, he removed himself from inside of me and saw the blood. He looked at me and said, "You weren't lying you were a virgin." In my mind I was saying, "Wow, Sherlock, you couldn't feel that?" He didn't apologize, he just told me to get dressed. Get dressed??? I didn't even know how I was going to get up and walk, much less get dressed! I laid there throbbing and began begging my body to behave. I muscled up the strength to get up and get dressed and then I heard those familiar words "Don't tell nobody. We have to keep this between us." I knew he was right nobody would protect me anyway, plus, my dad would be mad. From that moment, I belonged to him. He had put his stamp on my soul. I resolved to keep this secret and he took me to the home where my roommates were. I clearly remember not being able to look at any of my roommates in their eyes because I knew if I did, they would know. I took a bath, but it wasn't enough to wash away my sin, so I went to the host family's pool and swam all night trying to get cleansed. That didn't work "God, are you there?"

After the tour, I got to go home for a few weeks. I wanted to tell my dad, but I didn't want to rock the "family of God" boat not to mention, the friendship boat. To make matters worse, over the summer, my boyfriend broke up with me. It was like he knew I had betrayed him and he was right. He was a good guy and I didn't see the need to drag him into that mess. Was God punishing me again for someone else's sin?

I wasn't excited when it was time to go back to school; although I did miss my friends. I persuaded myself to just "suck it up" and finish strong. At that point, I was so elated that Southwestern was only a two-year program which meant I only had to get through one more year.

When I got back to school, I was different. My mom brought me a lot of new clothes and now that I was a woman, my walk and my talk had changed I had matured. My ex boyfriend noticed and wanted to rekindle our relationship. I tried to play hard to get but, honestly, I was glad I needed his protection.

Even through everything I had experienced, I was still named Who's Who Among Junior Colleges. I was an honor student and a section leader in the choir. My grades and involvement solidified that I was eligible to be a candidate for Miss Southwestern 1988. I ran for the tide and I was crowned I was the queen. A part of me felt like Ms. America. I was smiling but, little did anyone know, I felt like a liar and a hypocrite. Nevertheless, I walked, waved, and smiled as if everything was okay. I was used to pretending and at that time, I had become a master of it.

Throughout the year I had to put on my disguise. I was the "Queen" and I was the mistress. I made the mistake of thinking that I was being loved by my father's friend and I thought I was in love with him and was just keeping my boyfriend to cover up any suspicion. I even had the audacity to think he would leave his family for me I was tripping. This man was a well known evangelist with a family and he was not going to give that up for me. I can't tell you the pain I experienced watching him with his wifc and children. I wanted to take her place until one day he called me and told me he would never leave his family he had too much on the line. There I was parading around as queen, but felt I was being dethroned. Who did I think I was? I was to everyone this kindhearted, gifted, beautiful and smart woman, but I was caught up in a crazy web of lies and one night, it all came to a head.

My boyfriend and I had gotten into a fight and I needed the touch of my lover, but he was at home with his family. I felt alone so much so, I wanted to die. I just couldn't continue to live like that so I went into my room and wrote "I want to die" on my right hand. I went to a friend's room and asked her for some pain medicine and when I left her room I took the whole bottle. As I found myself drifting to sleep, my spirit emerged and changed my mind. I tried to holler out to my roommate, but I couldn't get my mouth to form the words. I managed to get some sound out of my mouth and by the grace of God my roommate heard my mumbles. She said, "Tonya, did you say something"? I couldn't answer I just stretched out my hand. She screamed, grabbed me out of the bed, and called out for my friend the one who had given me the pills. They immediately took me to the bathroom and tried to get me to throw up. Before I knew it, a circle had been formed around me and someone had turned me upside down trying to get me regurgitate the pills. They knew they couldn't allow me to lay down so, after several failed attempts to get me to vomit, they got me dressed to go outside to get some fresh air. It was close to curfew and no one should have been going outside, but when we got outside, people began to stare. My friends just said I was sick. You see, if it had gotten out, it would have been an automatic expulsion from school. The reason they didn't dial 911 or call for an adult to help is because they were trying to protect me the queen.

My college big brother was on the security team and when he asked what was wrong with me, they began making up stuff, until I told them it was okay to tell him the truth. My big brother told them "he had me" and would keep them updated. They went back into the dorm and my big brother took me for a walk around the campus and we walked and we kept walking. As we walked, he started crying and said, "Tonya, what about me? What about all the people who love you?" I didn't have the energy to explain all I could say was, 'Tm sorry". We walked some more and every time I tried to stop, he would snatch the back of my shirt and lift me off the ground so high that my feet dangled in the air he was not playing with me! He was not going to let me stop and was determined to keep me awake. We walked until it was morning and then he brought me back to my dorm room, letting my roommate know it was okay for me to go to sleep.

Now, remember, if this incident got out, I would be expelled, but of course it did. I knew there was no way everyone would be loyal. The word got to my father's friend who immediately came to the school and was granted special permission to come to my room. He knocked, entered, and sat on my bed expressing his feelings for me. Because he was on the staff, he knew the procedure. I would have a meeting with the dean, so he coached me on what to say so I wouldn't get expelled. I did exactly as I was told to do I lied so well I convinced the dean that the events of the night before didn't even happen.

If you know anything about Southwestern, it's a small school where everybody knows everybody. I knew the story got out and I would have to face it. I went to the cafeteria for the last meal of the day and when I entered, everyone stopped and stared you could have heard a pin drop. I was so ashamed, but I knew I had to keep walking and in time, everything would go back to normal.

I made it through the last months of that semester unscathed. Well, not emotionally. I knew if the church walls could not testify, the school walls sure wouldn't. Here existed another Christian place to keep my secrets. "God, are you there?"

I couldn't wait for graduation. I was ready for my family to come and take me back home. I graduated with honors and wore my yellow rope proudly. No one knew if I could have tied a knot in that rope I would have, yet I smiled and walked across the stage. I was praying to God and begging Him to make me better.

CHAPTER 4

"The Church Was

My Corner"

When you pray, you better know what you're praying for because God hears you. He will send you the test to see if you are sincere. I felt I was ready God had rescued me again. I returned home determined to put all the past behind me. For the moment I was free and I had survived another monster.

By the way, I didn't have time to think about me. My sister was about to bless our family with a baby girl. I had to make sure I protected her with my life. She would NOT go through what I had gone through I would be there to look out for her. Even though I wasn't physically carrying her, in my heart and emotionally I did. She would be another baptism my new start. If I could guard her from all the evil, God would finally reward me and take away all my pain. I prayed that her birth would cleanse me and I pledged to be the best auntie ever she would be my redemption.

On July 9, 1989, Kimberly Nicole Palmer graced us with her presence. I counted her fingers and toes she was so beautiful. She had a head full of hair and was perfect I had another living baby doll.

I was doing great at being an Auntie. If I had my way, she would never want for anything. I made a pact with God since He gave me another chance, I would never fail Him in that way again. I knew I couldn't be perfect, but my body would belong to Him. I was going to be a super Christian and I put my all into being good. I even began to buy into this family of God thing. The church was growing Southside had become a pillar in the community. We had the best choir on this side of heaven and I was proud of how God was using my father and our family. For the first time since I was a child, I felt I would make it. God was hearing my prayer, I was being good and I was living clean. I began to be relaxed in my walk, thinking, "I got this! I am good" . . . so I thought. That was the very mindset the devil was waiting for me to have. He knew I was getting comfortable in that new walk and was aware I was beginning to let my guard down.

I can't tell you how my next fall from grace actually started, but the devil definitely had my number. He knew I was determined to trust God to heal my hurt, yet he also knew my weakness I LOVED attention; and not just any attention male attention.

I can admit I was physically beautiful. I was aware of the power of my smile, my eyes, my breast, my long legs and my walk. I had mastered walking in heels the higher the better. My senses were keen; I knew when, where, who and what. I had proof from an early age that men were weak. I know the Bible says women are the weaker vessel, yet many men have fallen blinded by their vision they see what they like and they go for it. I was also aware that, being a preacher's daughter, I had access to the men of God that the average member didn't. I had, if you will, a V.I.P. pass behind the veil. The congregation saw them in the pulpit, but I had a close up view of their lives and ears to their conversations. Of course, not every single preacher had a weakness for women, but most of them did. I also understood that not only did I have access to them, they had access to me. I swear they could smell the stench of low self-esteem, worthlessness, and loneliness all over me. I was so easy to hook; I craved attention and it was so obvious to see.

I was also good at nurturing and had always been good at making people feel better. Even today, if someone comes to me hurting, by the time they leave my presence, they are full of hope and joy. I pride myself on that I am good at helping people see what is possible when they feel no hope.

One day I found myself in a conversation that I clearly see now was a setup by the devil. A gentleman in our close circle, who was 15 years my senior, was hurting because he and his lady friend had broken up. At 20 years old, I didn't know what advice I thought I could share with him, but I thought it was cool that he assumed I was mature enough to handle his storm. I was happy that he chose me out of everyone else to talk to. He trusted me. Can you say DUMB? I fell headfirst into that trap. We became close friends and I found myself talking to him every day. One day, he asked me to come over because he wanted to talk in person. He didn't live too far from the family, it was still early, so I said, "Sure".

When I got there, he began sharing more about the situation with his lady friend. He knew he had messed up and felt there was no way she would come back to him he was so sad. At this point, the Holy Spirit was shouting "RUN!!!" but instead of listening to the Holy Spirit, I did what he required of me I made him feel better. Yes, I slept with him. That continued for months church, fellowship with the family and sex that was our routine. The next thing I knew, he and his lady friend decided to get back together and she let me know where I stood, so I stayed away. Soon after they married to live happily ever after.

There I was alone again. I was heartbroken because I had given my total self to another man who was unavailable that became my lifestyle. I was doing ministry; however, it was ministry that was not authorized by God or Southside Church of Christ. I was a committee of one. If a church leader needed comforting, I was at their service. I gave "overtaken in a fault" new meaning. I could no longer call my lifestyle a mistake. I could no longer blame my molesters I was making a conscious choice.

I wanted to be loved and I was messing up royally and every time I got caught up in some mess, I prayed the most familiar prayer in the world

.

. . "Lord, if you can get me out of this, I PROMISE I won't do this again." God would always keep His end of the bargain, but I would not. Sex became like a drug to me. Those church soul ties were very hard to shake. Sex had become a shackle and shackles are very restrictive. They help to facilitate a mindset of limitation. They control you.

Church had become a place conducive to serve my craving. I had developed habits that made me feel like scum. These habits quickly turned me from a lady to a tramp. Porn became my bible, sex was my god and my flesh became my compass. The only time I felt good was when I was on my back. It's crazy, but there were times I would try to stop but my body would go through withdrawals. I was just like any other addict.

I remember the time when there was a revival at church and the preacher had his eye on several of us. He went to one of the brothers he could trust and let him know which one of us he was interested in. After discussing our differences and what was preferred, I was NOT his top choice I was just in the running. He didn't want to complicate his relationship with my father and felt it would be less problems if he could be with one of the other women. The brother informed him that out of his choices the ONLY one he knew for sure that would oblige him was me. Needless to say, the brother gave me all the information, and I went.

Isn't that the saddest thing you ever heard? I wasn't even top choice, but I was a sure choice and just like everyone before him, he climbed on top of me and I said "Amen." I remember closing his door as I made my exit and I just cried. What had I become? The very thing that I should have been running from I was running to. I collapsed in the hallway and cried I was wretched and undone.

After that night I understood that the only difference between me and the lady out there on the street, was where we stood. She may have walked the streets and had a corner, but the church had become my corner. I was no safer or smarter than her. At least she had enough sense to get paid. The only thing I received was a bad reputation. I wasn't even more saved than her. I was her! The church was my corner, and it was at that revelation I knew I had to change.

CHAPTER 5

"My Soul is DEAD"

I wanted a new life. I wanted an escape from that family of God thing, again. Church had become a joke to me. God was a fictitious character like Santa Claus and the Easter Bunny. Church was Halloween all year long. It was the place we gathered, all masked up and wearing our costumes of praise. We sang, prayed, and said "amen" to a God we had no intention of surrendering to. No one in my close world was transforming their lives they were merely performing tasks. I, too, had become a performer. I was so tired of bleeding and worshipping through my wounds. Whatever makes you bleed is your cross church was my cross.

I was so ANGRY! I wasn't even sure if it was possible to heal in the same atmosphere that made me sick. Was there any hope for me? Did Christ die for me too? I desperately wanted to release myself from the prison of negative, toxic, and destructive behavior. The thoughts of myself was killing me. I realized that I had bought into every single lie the devil told me since I was a child. I had a damaging assessment of myself and believed I was not enough. I thought I was worthless, filthy... nothing. I was on such a vicious cycle. I didn't love myself, but sex made me better then after sex, I felt like scum. I would repeat this merry go round over and over and understood I was at war with myself and no one else. I resolved that my life would be just one bad choice after another. Would I always be drawn to the forbidden? I felt my soul was not only trapped it was dead.

I reflected on the moment when, as a child, my soul died. I had been fighting to live again but believed I had become emotionally paralyzed by all the sexual abuse and all the sex I chose to have. The devil was doing everything he could to kill me, and I decided he was right about me. I was hopeless who would want me who could even love me?

I met my first husband at the church. He was charming, had a great speaking voice, was a track star, and he made me laugh. He was interested in getting to know me better so we began dating. He didn't have much financially, lived in a terrible neighborhood, and really didn't have much to offer me. I had a decent job and helped him pay his bills. I recognized that pattern and, in so many ways, I was paying him to love me. While we were dating, I had to travel a lot with ASAP (Acapella Singers Adding Praise). He would come along but would always be so possessive. If any man would shake my hand and say they enjoyed the concert, he would think they were coming on to me. If I responded in-kind, I was flirting. I had to keep explaining that I was just being cordial and was doing nothing wrong, but he would make it difficult for me on the road. I began to avoid greeting the audience and would just stay close to him. I confused his control with love and truth is I was offering a whole lot of excuses for his behavior.

After dating for over a year, he asked me to be his wife. I was 22 years old and I was elated because no one had ever wanted me for keeps. I was going to belong to someone I was going to be a bride. I had convinced myself that he would get better once we became husband and wife. I remember the day my father said, "Tonya, he is going to become worse once you are married." I responded, "Daddy, that doesn't make sense. I will be his wife. I will be coming home to him every day. That will prove to him I am totally his." I dismissed my father's warning and kept planning the wedding. As the days got closer to the wedding, he seemed to accuse me of everything. I kept trying to convince him that I loved him and I wouldn't hurt him, but I was so desperate to be loved that I was ignoring all the signs.

There were so many times I wanted to call off the wedding. What my father told me was beginning to make sense. My spirit was telling me no, but I didn't want to disappoint him or anyone else. I had two bridal showers and a bachelorette party but I wasn't happy. All I really felt was fear, but the fear of being alone was stronger than the fear of losing my life.

On August 1, 1992, I took the leap and got married. As my father walked me down the aisle, I became sick to my stomach. My bouquet was shaking perversely and I knew why. My whole body was shaking like a leaf. My dad asked, "Are you sure?" I nodded yes, but secretly hoped my dad would have taken me out of there. People had come from far and near and I didn't want anyone to be mad at me for not going through with the wedding. I put everyone else's emotions in front of my own. He had so many family members come in and it would have been embarrassing if I didn't get married. It was also my 23rd birthday, so we could have turned the reception into a birthday party, but I didn't. We exchanged vows and I pretended to bc happy.

The wedding was beautiful and it seemed everyone was enjoying it, but I saw the moment my father wiped tears from his eyes. He knew is his spirit I was making a mistake and he prayed that I would be safe. This was definitely a time he didn't want to be right. The reception was AMAZING!!! My husband and I thanked everyone for coming. We had joy in our hearts and looked forward to building our lives together.

We had a nice apartment, thanks to a couple who cosigned for us. I didn't have any credit and he had bad credit. I had vowed to them that we would not miss a payment. We didn't have much furniture and decided we would fill up one room at a time. I kept a clean home, loved to cook and we had a very healthy sex life. We both had full time jobs, but most of all I was happy to prove to him that I loved him. I was wearing his name and I prayed that gave him security. Things were going great! The next month came without any incidents and it appeared that I was right he just needed me to marry him and his jealousy would stop. I was glad that I didn't let fear win.

One evening as we were riding home from church, we came to a stop light. We were talking and as we sat at the light, I turned and looked at the vehicle beside us. When the light turned green, he quickly took off. Our conversation stopped. I asked him what was wrong, but he wouldn't respond. I couldn't imagine what I had done so I kept asking what was wrong and he just ignored me. As we approach our door, he grabbed me, pushed me against the wall, and began to strangle me. He strangled me off my feet and as I was gasping for air, trying to loosen his grip from around my neck, he dropped me down just before my breath was gone. I was crying and I stayed in a kneeling position as he began pacing saying, "You are not going to disrespect me. I will kick your ass! Don't you ever do that again!" I didn't have the energy to look up as I whispered as loud as I could, "What did I do?" He said, "Don't act dumb you know what you did." I insisted that I didn't and he said, "When we were at that stoplight, you looked over to the car beside us and you were staring at the man in the car." I couldn't believe I was about to die over a stranger in a car over a person who I would never see again, but he was so insecure. As my father's words began to echo in my head, I couldn't believe what had just happened to me. I was used to sexual abuse, but I didn't think I would ever have to encounter physical abuse by my own husband. Instead of calling 911 or my family, I decided that I would be okay. I decided not to look at anyone else and disrespect him. I told him I was sorry and it wouldn't happen again and he also apologized and told me that he loved me. He began to kiss me and we made love.

The next morning, I acted as though the events of the previous evening didn't happen. I told myself to make sure I didn't disappoint him again. Well, if you know anything about physically abusive relationships, you also know that no matter what the victim does or does not do, the abuser will find a reason to attack. I found myself at his mercy every day.

I didn't want to tell anyone, but my posture was clearly one of an abused woman. My family, friends and congregants would ask me all the time if I was okay, but just like an abused woman, I lied. I reverted back to what I had mastered in church I smiled and pretended to be okay. I found myself again asking, "God, are you here?" . . . and just like that, my soul died again. "God, why don't you just go ahead and kill me." This is the worst thing I could go through. I thought nothing could be worse than being abused by the man who says he loves you. I should have known by now that if it could get worse, it would. I was really about to find out.

CHAPTER 6

"My Lifeless Womb"

I can't tell you how many times I found myself in the path of my first husband's anger. The more I tried to make him happy, it appeared the angrier he became. I even asked him what I could do to make things better. I had a checklist to make sure I stayed on top of things: keep the house dean; cook every day; give him good love; work and provide. I loved Jesus, I was beautiful, a size 6, gifted and intelligent what else could he want?

He was a manager at a big drug store chain and with our combined monies, our bills were easily paid. We were almost three months into our marriage when he came home with some terrible news he had gotten fired. That news was devastating enough, but the reason he lost his job broke me. He was fired for sexual harassment. What??!!! It was bad enough that now all the bills would fall on me, but being fired for sexual harassment was too much. It was bad enough I was taking the beatings, but this?? He had not only put us at risk in a major way, but he had also put the couple who cosigned for our apartment in jeopardy. How could he be so selfish? I couldn't understand why he would do something so foolish.

I wanted to leave him, but you know what they tell you at church God hates divorce. Besides that, I didn't want to bring any shame to my father. What would people think and say if his daughter's marriage didn't work? I remembered how cruel some of the congregants were when my sister became pregnant out of wedlock. It had also been drilled into my head that there was only one reason to get a divorce, and that reason was adultery. I felt stuck. God didn't say I could leave because of domestic violence or did He? I asked God if He was punishing me because I felt I must have done something to deserve what was happening. Why did God hate me so? I was trying my very best to love this man, and his heart didn't work well, not towards me anyway. I regretted every day that I didn't listen to my father.

I was now the sole provider for our home and too embarrassed to tell anyone, so I just worked hard and took up his slack. I wanted to keep my vows I said for better or for worse and for richer or poorer. I thought to myself, "We should still be honeymooning. This is too soon for all of this". I also felt the weight of making sure that nice couple kept their great credit score I persevered.

Every day was a fight. He would beat me, then say he's sorry. I would forgive him and we would make love. I am in another vicious cycle. While all this was going on, I was still doing ministry. Sundays and Wednesdays felt like field trips. They were the only days I was able to see my family. He would quote that "leave and cleave" scripture to his advantage. Looking back, I knew people saw me dying. I had become a shell of myself and whenever I was questioned, I did what I had learned as a child in church I lied. I had the masked thing down to a science I would be in TERRIBLE pain but I made excuses. I would get angry at people for asking me if I was okay. I had to keep up a facade after all, God was punishing me and I was getting what I deserved. No one would be able to help me escape the wrath of God and I was resolved to the fact that no one could.

I was so thankful for those trips with ASAP because they gave me a reprieve from the beatings. During those moments, life was normal. I can't tell you how many times I wanted to say something, but I kept silent. I had become so used to the toxic cycle that I felt nothing I had become numb. Then there were times I would try to make love to him, but it was so painful; something was happening to my insides. It felt like my stomach was on fire and I would become so nauseated, but whenever I complained, he beat me. He accused me of sleeping with other people which astonished me because I wasn't. How could I be doing anything with anyone? There was no way I could have he kept me on a tight rope and knew where I was all the times. Besides, I knew he was capable of killing me. I would never do anything like that. For once in my life I was doing right.

It was my hope that things would get better. I was hoping that some of my father's sermons would start to prick his heart, because I can tell you, there is nothing like seeing the husband that is abusing you participate in worship. When he led the prayer, I couldn't say amen. If he read the scripture, I couldn't look at him. If he served on the communion table, I felt we were taking it in vain. It was my hope that him fellowshipping with the brethren would soften him.

One Sunday evening after returning home from an ASAP trip, I was exhausted and was hoping that we would have a peaceful night. It had become a pattern that whenever I came back from a ministry trip, he was even more evil. I guess it was because I travelled so much, but this would be a night I would never forget. I walked into my home and things were unusually peaceful. He hugged me and said he missed me. I enjoyed his kindness, but I couldn't help but wonder, "Who is this stranger in my house?" He looked like my husband, but he definitely wasn't acting like him. I remember being excited because hopefully I wouldn't get beat that night. I didn't like anything out of place, so I would normally unpack immediately, but this particular night he told me that he missed me so bad and told me to go ahead and take a shower. I smiled and ran into the bathroom tonight could be the turnaround for our marriage. When I got into the bathroom, I noticed a prescription pill bottle on the sink. I picked it up and read the label it had his name on it and the date of the prescription was from the weekend. I opened the bottle to look at the pills and I stepped out of the bathroom with the bottle and asked what happened while I was gone. He grabbed the bottle from me and told me that it was for a bad cold, but that he was feeling better and he urged me to get into the shower because he wanted to show me how much he missed me.

I was singing in the shower, smiling and was so happy that we weren't fighting that night. I came to bed in full anticipation of a hot night of passion. We hadn't been this way in a very long time and then it happened. He entered me and my stomach felt as though it was full of blood and fire. In my head I was hollering **"NOOOOOOOO NOT TONIGHT!!"** I can't feel bad tonight I won't complain of the pain tonight I will ignore the pain I can't mess up this moment. Tears were running down my face but I dare not ask him to stop. When he was done he rolled over and fell asleep. After he began to snore, I tried to get up and go to the bathroom, but I was in so much pain in my abdominal area I couldn't move I was nauseated again. What was happening to me? I dealt with the pain for months, but I kept pushing. He found another job and after I paid out the lease, we found something more reasonable and moved. It was nice and I was happy that I would be closer to the church and my family. This was our new start so I hoped.

I loved Sundays. Southside Church of Christ, affectionately known as "Holy Ghost Headquarters," was the place to be. We praised and worshipped because we knew God was definitely there. Oddly, on this Sunday, my husband didn't have a worship assignment and was able to sit with me I was elated. We had a visiting preacher and he was amazing. He preached the paint off the walls. The spirit was so high, and there were several that rededicated their lives to Christ. I noticed that my husband wasn't feeling what we were, but I kept praising. As the men served communion, I observed that my husband's jaws became tight, but I didn't question him.

Our church was not one of those that scattered after the benediction. We were big on fellowship and could easily be there for another thirty minutes to an hour after the service was over fellowshipping, but on that Sunday, as soon as the prayer warrior said "In Jesus' name, Amen," my husband grabbed my arm and said, "Let's go!" I could tell by the look in his eye and the tone in his voice, it was going to be a bad day.

When we got to the car I was angry because I didn't have an opportunity to speak to my family and friends. There would be no fellowship meal with them that day and as we were leaving the grounds, I asked him what was wrong he didn't answer. What could have set him off in worship? We get home and like clockwork, he grabbed me and slammed me against the wall saying I had disrespected him. I was dumbfounded because I was in worship. What could I have possibly done that was disrespectful? Sobbing, I begged him to stop beating me and was asking what I had done his answered floored me. He told me that when I said "amen" in a certain part of the sermon, it was obvious I was thinking about him. He also said that when the gentleman came with the communion tray, I looked up and smiled at him. Are you serious? I was getting beat for worshipping. Routinely, I would say "I'm sorry," he would say he was sorry, cry and apologize and I would console him but this time, I was enraged.

The beatings became too much and I had to tell somebody, so I finally opened up to my family. My father told my husband that he didn't give me to him to beat on me and told me I could come back home. I went to stay with my family I needed to figure out what I was going to do. That was the beginning of the back-and-forth journeys between my house and my parents' house.

On one of the occasions when I was staying with my parents, I became very ill. I made it to the emergency room and when they took me back, I could barely walk. Once they placed me on the bed, I started vomiting profusely and the staff worked desperately to get it under control. I was afraid I was dying. They gave me an IV and ran numerous tests and after a few hours they were able to rule out some things although it would be later when I would get the other results. I left that day without an answer.

During that week I decided to go back to my husband, hoping again to make our relationship work. I told him about my scare and he was grateful that I was feeling better. Later that week I received a letter from the emergency room doctor informing me of my illness chlamydia. I didn't have a clue what that was. Back in that day, there was no Google to look it up. I went to pick up a sister friend of mine and when she got in the car, I showed her the letter. She said, "Oh my God, Tonya"! He gave you a disease." I was in shock and I was angry. I called the number on the letter and the nurse confirmed what my friend told me and asked me where I wanted them to send in my prescription. I drove in complete silence to get the medicine and once I received the prescription I opened the bottle. I stood in the middle of the aisle completely astonished - these were the same pills he had months back. He knew he was sick and he purposely gave it to me. How cruel! I learned that if I had been treated in time, the antibiotics could have cured it, but the disease had been in my body for months. I also learned that one of the long term affects of the disease was a lifeless womb.

He wasn't there when I returned home so I waited in the living room with the letter and pill bottle on the table. When he entered, he knew something was wrong. I didn't say much at first. I let him read the letter and I showed him the pills. Before he could say a word, I asked "how could you do this to me?" I was completely crushed because he knew how desperately I wanted to be a mother. He knew all those times I said my stomach was hurting, I was being truthful. He knew every time he would beat me and said I was faking so I wouldn't have to have sex with him, he was the reason. I asked how he expected to heal when he was still having sex with me knowing he gave it to me. I then asked the big question Who did he cheat with? I told him that I had taken his beatings, but this is too much! YOU STOLE LIFE FROM ME! My womb is lifeless! He admitted he had contracted the disease from a woman he met on his route. I couldn't believe it he didn't think enough of me to wear a condom? He didn't even know her he met somebody one day and slept with them. This was totally unfair! He told me he was sorry and started crying I was not moved.

I had my out. The church said adultery was the only path to divorce and I was surely going to take it. I had a conversation with an older married woman who was very spiritual and I knew she had experienced infidelity. I really needed some solid spiritual advice and told her what happened. She and her husband had worked their situation out, but this was different my husband had killed my womb. She was sorry about what had happened to me. I told her about the beatings and everything. I was waiting for her to tell me to leave him, but instead she said, "In marriage, things happen. Men will be men. Now that he knows he has been caught, you can get anything you want from him. Since he has failed you miserably, you will get anything your heart desires." In my head I said, "What the hell??!! Is everybody crazy!!!" That was not what I expected from her but, honestly, I had seen other women at church with that same posture. The man gets to do what he wants, he says he is sorry and buys something nice. The bible tells you to forgive, and you repeat in that order.

I drove back home thinking maybe this was just another punishment. It would look crazy if I got divorced so soon. Maybe I was the crazy one. Even though I felt I'd be better off dead, I told him it was okay I would find a way to work it out. Then that famous lie (oops, I mean line) came out of my mouth "Honey, I forgive you." You would think things would get better, but not too long after that, the beatings were back. He became so paranoid he didn't want me to sing anymore. He didn't want me to go to church or to my family's house. He wanted to isolate me from everyone that loved me. For a period of two years, I went back and forth between my home and the home of my parents.

I went back to him after receiving the same promises and each time I thought things would change. One day he came home in a bad mood. I must have said something that set him off more. The next thing I knew he had grabbed me and body slammed me to the ground. I immediately knew this injury was different I felt paralyzed, but I knew I had to try to get up. As I tried to get up, he stomped me in the face saying, "Nobody is going to want you but me. You're fat and you're ugly." I knew he had lost his mind. I definitely wasn't ugly and I was a size 6, but who cared what he thought, I had to find a way out of there. He must have heard my thoughts because he took my keys so I couldn't drive away. I noticed the front door was unlocked and made a decision to run. I ran to a neighbor's house and luckily they were home. They called the police and he was arrested. I went to the hospital and my ribs were injured and I had to get crutches. I remember looking in the mirror wondering, "How did I get here?" I knew if I didn't make a decision to leave, the next time they could have been rolling my body into my father's church to be viewed. That was the day I decided to save myself. I went back to my father's house, filed for divorce, and after three years of marriage, I was free from him. I was free from him, but I wasn't free from myself and my lifeless womb. Who would want me now?

CHAPTER 7

"Addicted to Love"

Love and I had a very toxic relationship. As I stated earlier, I truly believed that love and sex were synonymous. No sex no love. In addition to having no one to love (sex) me, now I had a womb that didn't function properly. I felt as though I was not a woman. I would never hear the heartbeat of a child, therefore I felt as though my heart had stopped beating. I had no hope and I wasn't looking towards the future.

What kind of future would I have without love, sex, and a baby?

I had a routine and ritual that I was thankful for. I had to be in the presence of the Lord on Sunday, but I was feeling embarrassed and ashamed. For years, I had been pretending to be well when I was sick so it was nothing for me to smile and make believe I could feel God's presence for two hours. Hell, I had been doing that since I was six. This time, I knew it would be harder than ever.

Have you ever walked into an assembly, and everyone stopped and stared? I heard the whispers as I walked by. I was walking but my legs were as limp as cooked noodles. My body felt like one big weight and my feelings about praising a God who allowed life to be taken from me was confusing. I was very familiar with John 10:10, but I felt God was the one killing, stealing and destroying. I began to question the realness of this abundant life God promised me. I was taught that God couldn't lie, yet I felt He did. I was beyond despair but I was still hoping God would show up. One thing I knew for sure, where the people of God meet, the devil is in attendance as well.

There was this family who became dose to our family. They lived far from the building but insisted on making the long drive each Sunday to worship. They began to come to our home between services so they wouldn't have to make the tedious journey back and forth. Before long, the father, an inspiring preacher, had become a vital part in the leadership at church. The family, as a whole, was very faithful. He was proficient in the work of the church and I loved the whole family. Their relationship with our family was in semblance to our closeness to the Jackson family in Jacksonville, Florida. They had small children who I would love on as if they were my own. They didn't know it, but they were therapy for me.

Things were going great until there became a mutual attraction between the father and me. He was nine years my senior but very easy to talk to. He wasn't judgmental of my past and he didn't condemn me for my confusion about God. He became my close friend. We found ourselves on the phone for hours each day and the next thing I knew we wanted each other in every way. I really adored his wife and I didn't want to hurt her, so even though I was feeling him, I fought the attraction. I would argue with myself about not going back to being a mistress and even though I was hurting, I knew sleeping with another married man in church wouldn't make me feel better. I struggled with not entertaining the thought of us.

You know that scripture about the "spirit is willing but the flesh is weak"? well I can testify that it's true. Emotionally and spiritually I was already having an affair. It was only a matter of time when the physical would manifest. It's crazy how your flesh will have you rationalizing your bad behavior. I actually said to myself, "Girl, you have been keeping secrets all your life. At least he treats you like he loves you. After everything you've been through, you deserve someone loving you." What a foolish disposition!! I justified why I had to give myself to him. He was patient, gentle, kind and my friend. It didn't feel as if he was using me. This felt good and right. I made a choice to make love to him.

That affair lasted for two years. I even moved out of my parents' home and got my first place so he could come and go as he pleased. There were times when he had his children with him and when they were I pulled down my personal pictures so they wouldn't connect where they were. I had snacks for them and would put the TV on cartoons before they got there so they would be entertained because I knew I would be keeping their father busy. Can you imagine how low of a woman you would have to be to have children sitting in your living room while you are in your bedroom making love to their father?

What I didn't count on was him falling in love with me. We actually talked about running away together. We were so caught up. I would even take the whole family to dinner sometimes just to spend time with him when my family was unavailable. I started believing his children were mine. In church, they wanted to sit with me. I loved on them so much, I think they were even confused, but you know who wasn't confused? - his wife and my parents. It was obvious to them that something was going on. Of course when approached and asked if there was something going on I lied we both lied. We even decided to stop speaking for a moment so things could cool down, but that didn't last long we missed each other terribly.

The day came when his wife found a letter I had written to him. I was angry because he shouldn't have taken the letter into his home. STUPID! Then I knew there wasn't any way to maintain our relationship. It's funny when a man is caught, they will do what it takes to cover themselves.

I was alone once again. I became the blame for a man making his choice to sin. Everyone treated me like I was a Jezebel, but he just made a mistake. When his wife told him he couldn't be friends with me anymore, I fell into a deep depression and hated living without him, so I decided I didn't want to live.

On a Sunday afternoon, I decided I had enough of this life. It was Mother's Day and my brother Q was in town. I had dinner with my family and was expecting that it would be my last supper. I was so sad, but I didn't want them to see me cry. I said goodbye to my brother who was heading back to Virginia and I looked at the rest of my family and mentally said goodbye. I went into my room and wept. I grabbed my prescription bottle of pills and took them all. As I was drifting, my sister entered my room to return a sweater. She looked at me and immediately saw the empty bottle. She hollered for my dad and he ran up the steps. They put me in the car and my dad took me to the emergency room. The emergency room staff took me back and set up everything to pump my stomach. One of the attendants on the team knew me and was shocked to see me in that condition. He prayed over me and told me everything would be okay. The next thing I knew, I woke up. I thought once I was in recovery I would be released into my father's care, but I was wrong. They put me in an ambulance and took me to the mental care ward. They were having me admitted! I couldn't believe it. I was in the crazy house! That evening my mom, sister and niece came to bring me a bag for my stay. Reality didn't set in until they wouldn't allow my niece to come in. She was too young to come on the floor, so I had to wave to her through a small window. I began to cry because I wanted to hug my niece. The attendant did allow my mom to come into my room, but they had to search the bag she was bringing to me. They made two piles as they started taking things out thing I could keep and things I was not allowed to have. My mom brought me some can drinks, but I couldn't have them because I could use the tab to cut myself. They wouldn't let me have my curling iron either because I could burn myself. I couldn't have the clothes or shoes with strings because I could use them to strangle myself. Tears streamed down my face. Once they gave my mom the things I couldn't have she had to leave. I remember crying so hard because I couldn't go home. I didn't want my mother to leave me there, but I had to realize it was my actions that landed me there. The days there were hard. It was hard to rest because every 15 minutes, they came into my room to make sure I was not trying to hurt myself. Then there were the group meetings and the one on one sessions with the psychiatrist. Even though what I did could have turned out another way, after days with God, I knew He kept me here for a reason. I had no clue what the reason was, but I was thankful He didn't let me die.

Eventually I returned to church and I had to see my ex lover and his family for the first time. As usual, he was able to maintain his family. Shortly after my return to church, they moved away and he even became a pulpit preacher for a congregation. Tonya, when are you going to learn how this game works?

To help me occupy my time I decided to get a second job and I was working nonstop. I was beginning to find myself and for the first time, even though I was okay with not having a man to love, was I okay with not having a man to love me?

One Thursday afternoon, my friends from my morning job asked me to call in and go out with them that night. They were going to get some drinks and enjoy some karaoke, so I did just that I deserved to have some fun. I called my sister and some other friends to invite them to come. As we sat talking, laughing, and drinking, this tall, dark, and handsome young man approached our table. He was a friend and former coworker of my friends. I was immediately drawn to him. His conversation was intriguing

I was captivated. When I didn't think things could get better, he put his name in rotation for karaoke and chose to sing "Always and Forever" by Heatwave. He could really sing! In fact, he killed it and I was in awe. After the karaoke we danced the night away. As we were about to leave, he asked me for my phone number. I was elated. We had so much fun and I was old fashioned, so I wouldn't have asked him for his number. If he wanted to be in contact with me, he would have to pursue me. The next day he called and we instantly became an item.

About one month into our relationship, he told me that he had a baby on the way. My immediate response was to cut my losses because I didn't want to be in the way of his relationship. I was hurt but thankful I hadn't invested too much time in the relationship. As I was bowing out, he quickly explained that even though a baby was on the way, he was not in a relationship with the young lady and that he wanted to be with me.

I must admit I was relieved. I really loved him and this baby would be an opportunity for me to be a mom.

We started dating in April, 1996 and he began attending church with me. We enjoyed each other tremendously and I was beginning to laugh again. We could talk about anything and that was just what I needed.

His daughter was born December, 1996 and I was frantic. I would be lying if I told you I wasn't worried. I thought he would see his baby being born and decide he wanted to make a family with the baby's mother.

I just waited for the shoe to drop. I stayed at his apartment awaiting his arrival and when he came home, he immediately took me in his arms and let me know nothing had changed. I was his woman and he wanted us to remain. To say I was relieved is an understatement. Later that month he got baptized at my father's church.

He began traveling and singing with us. He had an amazing gift. He was a preacher's son and he was proficient in the word. We had similar journeys. He accepted me and my crazy past and understood perfectly the "behind the veil" trappings and mentality. I was thankful for him but I was having feelings of inadequacy. I wanted love, but felt underserving of it. I struggled with insecurity. I just didn't believe that a man could be faithful. I had never seen it and most of my journey consisted of unfaithful and unapologetic church men. He had to constantly reassure me and we got into arguments because I was always being accusatory - I didn't trust anyone.

One Sunday evening as I was directing the choir, the lyrics of the song touched me so deeply that it brought me to tears. I realized that I was a hot mess. I had no peace, I was angry, and I needed some major help. I decided that night that I was going to get therapy. I knew if I didn't get myself under control, I would be dead, in jail or in a mental institution. I also knew that I would lose my man if I didn't change.

I was excited yet nervous about going to therapy. When I shared with a trusted pastor that I was told going to therapy, he told me that therapy was a sin. I received all the church jargon and cliches about praying and trusting God how only He could help me and how my faith must have been weak. He went on and on. I responded by saying, "If therapy is a sin, I'm about to bust hell wide open because I really need help." He was a counselor himself and he knew firsthand I had tried all of that. He knew depression could not be prayed away and that you couldn't just sing and shout away the paralyzing affects of molestation. He knew you couldn't just hope away the pain of divorce and he also knew I had tried to numb it away with drugs, alcohol, and sex. Nothing was working and I was in desperate need of help.

God is so intentional. He had me assigned to a male therapist he knew the things I needed to hear and see would be more powerful if a man told and showed me. I was hesitant because I had never experienced a man in power not take advantage of me, but in spite of my reservations, I went to my appointment.

I was 28 years old. By this time, I had so much to unpack I had so many secrets. The more I shared with him the facts of my life, the more it sounded like a horror movie. I assumed that this man was going to remove himself from my case, but he patiently listened. He asked questions that provoked pure honesty. Even I, couldn't believe all the things I had suppressed. At the end of the session, he was honest about how hard the process would be. He shared with me that he was spiritual not religious, and he wanted to make sure I was comfortable with not having a Christian therapist since I was so rooted in religion. I smiled at him and said, "I am glad you are not a man in church because I wouldn't be able to trust you." He promised if I did the work, healing was possible.

Let me tell you, when he said the process would be hard, he wasn't kidding. Having to dig deep and regurgitate everything I had suppressed was quite often debilitating. After most of my sessions, my body was in pain and my head was throbbing and at times, I could barely walk. Thankfully, he had a masseuse on staff. I needed her as much as I needed him. Therapy was intense, but I can truly say it saved my life. One day he said those magic words, "Tonya, you are more than your body." WHAT???!!! I never thought I was anything but a body. He spoke of my intelligence and strengths and my resilience and tenacity. He spoke about my gift of honesty and my bravery. Those were descriptions of me which I had never heard. I can't express to you how hearing this from a man empowered me. He never mishandled me and he never abused his power he was solid. I am happy to say that we are still in touch with each other today. He has been my consistent cheerleader and I praise God for him.

In the summer of 1998, ASAP had a missions trip to Jamaica. We knocked on doors telling the natives about Jesus during the day and at night we held services under a tent. I was grateful for the days we had some down time. I really enjoyed Dunn's River Falls and shopping in the market. We were set to fly back home on my 29th birthday. As we took our seats, I saw several of the members of my group whispering to the flight attendant, but I took my seat. My seat and my boyfriend's seat were not together. My niece and I were in another row and as I got my niece settled, the flight attendant approached me and wanted me to switch seats with the passenger sitting next to my boyfriend. I said I would love that but I was not leaving my niece beside a stranger. She was only 9, so both passengers switched with us. As we reached the highest altitude, 35,000 feet, the pilot came on the intercom. He welcomed everyone to the flight then he said, "Today is LaTonya Stephens 29th birthday." He announced my seat number and said that my boyfriend had something very important to ask me. All eyes were on us. My boyfriend pulled out a ring and asked me to marry him. I screamed, cried, and said YES! The cabin exploded with applause. After we landed, everyone was passing by and congratulating us. When we approached the cockpit, the captain gave us a bottle of champagne with a big bow. I was so happy. I couldn't believe this was happening to me.

My boyfriend made it clear he was ready to get married and didn't want a long engagement, so on August 28, 1998, we married and had a beautiful intimate ceremony. I remember taking a moment just for God and me. I looked up and said, "To God be the glory."

I loved my second husband from the depths of my soul. I dreamed of being the best power couple in the world. Even though we were in ministry, we made our marriage a priority. The best times were when we were able to minister together. We were the best of friends, our communication was great and on Sundays we dressed alike. We were a real life black Ken and Barbie. We loved to dance and laugh and we complimented each other in every way.

I was healing and I was thankful that God gave me another chance at this love thing. I was beginning to trust. When you have been abused and suffer from childhood trauma, trust isn't easy. It was an uphill battle and even though I had been through intense therapy, I understood healing was a process. My life had been indoctrinated and cultivated by liars, cheaters, and bad behaviors; not just by others, but by my very own choices, so trust was going to require some work. I knew I couldn't get comfortable and relax and it would take time to grow and mature in this new love, but I wanted to be the best wife ever.

We both worked and shared household duties and he was an excellent cook. We had rules for the kitchen when one cooked, the other washed dishes. When it came to laundry, we both believed the process had to be complete you wash, dry, fold and put up the laundry in the same day. While I was OCD with the cleanliness, he could fix anything with his hands. I never had to call the plumber, auto mechanic or a handy man. He was a jack of all trades the Ying to my yang.

The more we travelled, the more popular he became. He became a worship leader at the church as his gift was definitely making room for him. People took notice especially females. I constantly had to remind myself that the only person I had to trust was him and I couldn't allow people to get into my head. We had certain rules before we entered a building to worship, we would make sure we displayed affection towards each other. We had to say we loved each another and after the benediction, the first fellowship hug had to be with one another. These were a must. If you know anything about triggers, you'll understand why these rules were in place.

We did well for a while, then I begin seeing things that I didn't like. I tried to dismiss them, but they manifested in my nightmares. I became increasing paranoid and I knew something was off because the whisper in my soul began speaking to me. So, I did what most Christian wives do, I ignored my feelings. I told myself I didn't see what I saw and I convinced myself I couldn't even trust my soul because there were too many holes in it. Plus, just as the older sister advised me before, men will be men. I had even resolved within myself that if something was going on, I deserved it because "you reap what you sow." While in therapy, I learned the first person you must trust and love is yourself. I learned to trust my instincts and to center myself. I learned the benefits of honesty; yet the first chance I had to see what life was showing me, I hid behind worship. What more could I do for God? It had to be something. I needed something else positive to drown out the negative whispers in my heart.

I started a gospel mime team and the ministry was powerful. It consisted of children and adults of both genders. The thing I really loved about that ministry was the fact that it was different and fresh. Every song was selected to encourage and admonish the saints. My father's church had never had a dance ministry. I believe there are many forms of ministry and told my father that sometimes he may not reach a person with his pulpit sermon, but God could use us to reach them through Mime Expression. Music has a way of touching the soul. We were requested to perform all the time and I began to see the church opening up to this ministry. I loved the way God was using me and my husband was my number one cheerleader. I noticed when I focused on God, I didn't have time to be distracted by negative thinking.

I was teaching the ladies bible class, writing for our church newsletter, miming, singing in several groups, and teaching the teenage young ladies bible class. In addition, I was a frequent speaker and workshop facilitator at different ladies' programs whatever God put in my hand to do, I was doing it.

On one particular Sunday, our church was in revival and the visiting preacher began to read a very familiar text he read the 23rd Psalm. I was 34 at the time and I can't tell you how many sermons I had heard from this text. However, I knew not to sign off mentally because the word is so rich and always unfolding. I was taught how to exegete scripture, therefore I was excited to hear his take on this passage. Ironically, the title of his sermon was, "A New Look at an Old Friend." It was as if he was reading my thoughts. One of the main things that stuck with me was the relationship between the shepherd and the sheep. The shepherd was the protector of the sheep. Sheep are dumb animals and, if not guided, they would wander away. Sheep also walked with their heads down. The shepherd knew there were hidden dangers that the sheep wouldn't see. He knew the field had holes and that snakes lived in the holes. In preparation for any attacks from the snakes, the shepherd would put oil in the holes so when the sheep were walking with their heads down and totally unaware of the danger, the snakes couldn't harm them. The snake would jump up to attack the sheep, but the oil would be slippery, causing the snake to slide back down into the hole and leaving the sheep unharmed. Just as Jesus is our ultimate shepherd, our pastors are to be our shepherds. It hit me like a ton of bricks that no one had ever put any "oil in the holes for me." It was then and there that I declared that in any ministry I was pastoring, if you will, I would make sure the "sheep" would have plenty of oil.

The year was 2006 and God was beginning to download visions to me. He had an assignment for me he wanted me to give voice and ministry to taboo subjects in church. He wanted me to be the face of surviving the dark side of the church. He wanted me to help others who were hurting. I told God NO! I wasn't about to do that, but He wouldn't let up. I shared the visions with my husband and He thought, with everything I had been through, I could help a lot of people, especially those who were dealing with church hurt. I shared that vision with three of my friends and they agreed, but I still didn't move. The day came when God and I began to wrestle daily. We were really at war. God kept urging me and I knew if I took the assignment, my world as I knew it would fall apart, so I kept saying NO! I knew God was going to win and I acknowledged that my arms were too short to box with God but I stood my ground.

One Sunday afternoon my spirit was heavy with sorrow and I couldn't figure out why. I was doing well so I thought. My husband and I had survived some serious issues, but I was determined to not go through another divorce and that I would weather any storm. We were in a good place. Normally, we would ride to church together but because he had something to do after service, we decided to drive separately. We entered the building and took our seats. I sat in the sanctuary and all I could feel was gloom. I was trying to praise but I couldn't. Nothing was physically hurting, but it was like my soul became paralyzed then I looked up and saw him. Walking behind my father was my father's friend heading to the pulpit preparing to preach. It was the preacher that took my virginity. I immediately began crying and my heart started beating real fast. I couldn't get my bearings. "Why is he here? Why is my father still friends with him? Why? Why? Why?" I couldn't get myself together. I listened as my father eloquently introduced him and I was crushed. When I started hyperventilating, my husband took me out and the nurse administered it to me. I was angry and I felt betrayed. Once I calmed down and caught my breath, I wanted to go home. There would be no worship service for me that night that was out of the question. My husband walked me to my car and I assumed he was going to get in his car, follow me home and take care of me, but he said he wanted to stay. I was outraged! That day, I knew I was alone and there was no covering for me. I sped off and called a pastor friend and mentor. I was crying uncontrollably. He comforted me and asked the same question I asked. "Why did my father let him come and preach in his pulpit"? He said he was going to contact my father and whatever he said to him worked because I have not seen him again since that day.

That incident was the reason I decided to tell God yes. The vision and assignment was clear so I set up a meeting with my father. We first talked about my feelings of betrayal and disloyalty and he apologized. He said he was unaware that his friend's presence would upset me because over the years I had been able to go to his church and perform, or see him and speak to him. I let my father know that I just did what everyone expected me to do be silent and smile. I also shared with him the vision God gave me and he loved it. There was just one problem he wanted me to share the vision with the head of the women's ministry and put the conference under their ministry. I didn't agree with that. God had entrusted me with the vision and I knew the church would water it down. I was determined to do it the way God instructed me to.

It took some time for me to organize it, but the "I Was Not Built to Break" Empowerment Conference was birthed in May, 2009 and it was a great success. Women loved a space that allowed them to be comfortable in their transparency. Of course there was some backlash because some believed the church was not a place to talk about molestation, abuse, toxic relationships and other subjects. I was all set for the backlash because just a year earlier I was a featured speaker at the National Ladies Lectureship where I made it clear that I would no longer be silent. My message was well received, even though some of the powers that be were angry.

At the very time I was successful with the conference, my husband and I were separated. I was dealing with so much emotionally and even though we were cordial, we knew our relationship had run its course. We kept trying, but too much had happened. We were dealing with addiction and infidelity, and we were both broken. He was a church leader and I knew I couldn't compete. At that time, and I confess, my attitude was, "If you can't beat them, join them." I said things like "What you can do, I can do better. Fool me once shame on you, but fool me twice and repeatedly, shame on me." So, I got into the game. During this time, I began a sexual and emotional relationship with a woman. I was what they call bicurious. I was so tired of being mistreated by men and thought that maybe a woman would treat me better. I didn't feel as though I was a lesbian but I was very appreciative of her care and friendship. It was nice to be desired and I could talk to her. With her, I experienced a feeling of safety I had never known. We knew the relationship couldn't last long because we both had attachments. I was still married. Even though my husband and I had open communication, we had both tasted the forbidden. I found some things on our computer and his phone. Women were mad at me because they weren't me. He could sense that something had changed and after a while, I admitted what I had done. That was a major shift. We all know men can't take what they put out, so needless to say, we were at a point of no return. After several attempts to reconcile our marriage, we gave up and our

CHAPTER 8

"God, what is Love?"

The bible says, "God is love, and whoever abides in love abides in God and God abides in Him." "God is love, and all who live in

love, live in God, and God lives in them." I was on an urgent quest to understand all of this. Could the reason I was ignorant of love be because I was ignorant of God?

There I was, 43 years old, reared in church, with a powerful ministry and my relationship with God felt like one big bipolar episode. There were the high highs and low lows. One day we were the best of friends and the next it seemed as though were enemies. I could be singing "Oh how I love Jesus" one moment and forsaking Him in the next.

As I pondered on my flawed and distained view of love, I thought about the times when my behavior was borderline schizophrenic. I hated the men at church who sexually abused me as a child, but as an adult, I willingly volunteered my body to the pulpit. It was like my altar to gain access to a God that was always mysterious to me. I remembered attending national church conferences year after year. A lot of the preachers would attend without their wives. It was known, especially after the night sessions, that many of them would be looking for a hook up. I would position myself in hopes of being picked. How crazy is that? As I stated earlier, the church was my corner. There aren't any words to articulate how nasty I felt. There I would be in a place of worship knowing after shouting "Amen", I'd soon be on my back participating in another type of worship. I would dance between sacredness and shamefulness and wouldn't miss a beat. I would give them my soul only to be left alone to fellowship with the scraps of Jesus' broken body.

I reflected on all the times I would vomit before entering and leaving church buildings. I wanted to be there to worship God, but having to face His men made me sick to my stomach. To this day I cringe when I hear the scripture "greet one another with a holy kiss," and I can't tell you how many times that passage was taken out of context. I was even aware that worship comes from the Greek word "proskuneo," which is translated to mean "kiss." That kind of affection only belonged to God, so why was it so easy for me to give God's love away?

I knew the only way to get the love I desired was to work diligently on my relationship with my Creator. I concluded, if my relationship with Him became healthy, I could finally have intimacy with myself. I acknowledged that I had a love hate relationship with myself because I had a love hate relationship with God. I praised Him for my gifts, intelligence, beauty, and heart, yet I hated Him for allowing the abuse, hardships, and trials. I knew I must let go of my anger and resentment towards Him. I was doing ministry in His name, but He and I weren't in a relationship.

I was no different than any other addict trying to numb their pain. Where the drinking, smoking, partying, and sex didn't work, I tried to pump church and ministry through my veins. Ministry was just another way to get a fix. How many committees could I be on? How many speaking engagements could I get? How many classes could I teach? I felt if I could just do ministry, it would drive my demons away. I thought if I shouted louder, danced harder and served tirelessly, God would show up and heal me, but you can't use praise as a band aid it must be your weapon. I was trying to cover my pain instead of surrendering it.

I knew until I could unite my spirit to His Spirit, I would never be at peace with myself. I desperately wanted that liberation which only comes when guilt and grace collide, so I began to pray. I needed Him like never before.

God do you love me? Can anybody love me? I remember looking towards heaven desperately waiting for a sign that I had the strength to survive another broken relationship. God and I had been here before, but the second divorce brought me to my knees. It's one thing to be free but it's another thing to be delivered. I was out of the marriage, but he wasn't out of my heart. If I am totally honest, I didn't know how to live without him he was my God.

As I made that confession, the words of my mother echoed in my ear. She told me a long time ago, "God is a jealous God." She also said, "Anyone or anything you put before God will disappoint you." Her wisdom had become my truth. I had spent 17 years addicted to a love that didn't and couldn't serve me. I came to my second husband in and on pieces. I surrendered to him as if he was my Savior and when he left, my pieces had pieces. After all the ministering I had done to and for others, I didn't have the strength to encourage myself.

As I grieved the loss of another marriage, I asked God to remove my definition of love. I begged Him to cut out any beliefs I had been indoctrinated with about love. I acknowledged that I didn't know the first thing about love and I became a blank canvas ready for Him to write on and in my heart. I not only needed to know what love was, but how should it operate.

In addition to becoming an empty canvas, I was open and honest with Him. I asked Him for an extra measure of strength to remain devoted to Him. I didn't want to be faithful to my body anymore. We both were aware that sex was my drug of choice. Therefore, I begged Him to take the taste out of my mouth. I didn't want my appetite for sex to continue to keep me from being the woman He created me to be. I was determined to be different and I hoped the devil would give up after a while but he wouldn't be the angel of darkness if he did. He was so patient and knew, at some point, I would relax. He just waited for me to get comfortable in my new walk, then he pulled out all his tricks. He knew me very well and he went below the belt. He knew I still loved my ex-husband and even though we were divorced on paper, we still had a strong passion for one another. He still was my best friend my soul tie. We would go out on dates and we talked all the time. He would even come to my city to fix things around my apartment and provide maintenance on my car. The familiarity of his attention brought me back to his bed. Oh no God, I'm sorry. A part of me had convinced myself that we were going to get remarried, so I started rationalizing my behavior.

My world crumbled when I found out that he and I were not on the same page. I had allowed my feelings for him to deepen but, to him, our marriage was a thing of his past. I remember hoping we would see each other on what would have been our one year anniversary apart. I wanted him, but he was on a plane on his way to visit someone else. That broke me, but that was my last day of living in my fantasy.

I went back to God and said, 'Tm for real this time." I was going to fight hard this time. I began to do the hard work on myself. No dating . . no men no sex. I did have a few hiccups with one man, then I became more disciplined. I would even call friends to come "baby sit" me when things got challenging. Once I started to truly see God, I got a glimpse of my true beauty. After failing numerous times, I finally got myself together and God was my only love. My body was finally His temple.

Being a Christian was not just my title, it was my lifestyle. I wasn't doing ministry to numb my pain anymore I had been redeemed. I was falling in love with Tonya and was even comfortable with the idea of never being in a relationship again. I was content with God being my man because I knew my heart was safe and in the best hands. My ministry was growing, I was at peace and thriving, and I had great girlfriends. I was good.

As I began to prepare for the 2016 "I Was Not Built to Break" Empowerment Conference, one of my team members suggested that I needed to get out. She was giving me her view on my consumption with ministry. She recognized my growth and was very proud of me; however, she said I needed to have some fun. When she asked me when was the last time I had a date, I told her that I dated myself all the time. I had learned how to take myself out. I went to the movies and dinner alone and I would even send myself flowers. I was good without a man. She encouraged me to "go out with a man if for nothing else, to get a free meal." I laughed and she told me she was going to set a profile up for me on this dating site. I was opposed to that because I was not about to pay someone to find me a mate. She said Plenty of Fish Dating Site was free.

She took my phone and put in all the information she knew, then told me to add pictures and the words for my profile.

In my profile there were some specific statements, such as: "I am a woman of God." "I am serious about Jesus and making heaven my home." "I don't have time for games." "You must have job and a car." One of the statements that I put in bold and capital letters was, "I DON'T WANT TO DATE A PREACHER!" I added some of my hobbies and goals and even shared my height preferences. I wore high, high heels and I wasn't interested on looking down to my man. My age range was 45 to 55 and even though I was 46 at that time, I didn't mind being a cougar to man a year younger.

The responses that I received were hilarious. You would think that men with my age requirement would have some class, but some of them didn't have the maturity of a 5-year-old. They told me how beautiful I was but then asked me to send them naked pictures. I hadn't been in the dating world for almost two decades so I assumed things had changed, but this was ridiculous. I was on that site for three days, but after so many nasty messages and unfruitful responses, I decided to remove my profile. As I was about to delete the profile, I noticed there was a new voice message. This message was from the man who would become my third husband. It was funny because the very thing I was adamant about, he ignored.

He had a wonderful voice and he loved Jesus too. He was a Christian, had a job and a car and seemed to be a good person but he was a preacher! I was not interested! I asked him if he had read my profile and he understood that I did not want to be with a preacher. He told me he was ordained but he didn't have his own church. He said he preached from time to time but wasn't interested in fulltime pulpit ministry. Praise the Lord! I didn't want to be rude, but I just wasn't interested in dating. The whole profile thing was a big mistake, but it allowed him an opportunity to talk me into one date.

On the day of the date, I was so nervous. I had forgotten how to date and people were crazy he could be a mass murderer. I was so hesitant, and I asked him to give me some specific information. I wanted his address, driver's license number, license plate, where he worked and where he was taking me. I downloaded his picture and sent it with all the information I had collected to three of my friends. I also sent them a picture of what I was wearing so if I went missing, they would have information to give to the police. When I arrived at my destination, I let my friends know I was not playing.

We met at the Olive Garden one of my favorite places to dine, and we had a good time. We had serious conversations about the preacher thing and the fact that I was not interested in living that life. We spent hours sharing very important things. He was 54 and I was 46, so we didn't have time for games. We talked for hours and when we were ready to leave, he asked me to come to his car. I panicked, but he assured me that I was safe. I walked with him and when I got to the back of his car, I stopped. He reached into his car and pulled out some roses. I thanked him and began laughing so hard. I said to him, "You wanted to make sure I was deserving of the flowers", then we left. I can truly say, it was nice being treated like a lady.

After dating for a few months, I decided that the relationship was not going to work for me. He was a nice man, but the connection I desired wasn't there. I didn't think it was right not have the same feelings. When I shared how I felt, it really hurt him and I felt bad, so I told him I would give it more time. I attempted to sabotage the relationship, hoping he would get fed up, but his decision was solid. I once tried to break up with him and as I was talking, he started praying. He told me he talked to God and he knew I was the woman for him.

God are you here? What should I do? For the first time, I was being treated with respect but I was not feeling what I thought I should. I reflected on my past and the truth is, I could never trust my feelings. Maybe I should be content with him just being a good person. At least he really loves Jesus. Maybe us both loving Jesus would be enough. Maybe I was just uncomfortable because I was used to toxicity. Maybe feeling passion was not necessary since it was what always got me in trouble anyway. I prayed for a good man, God sent him and I needed to be grateful. Plus, people were saying I couldn't keep a man and treated me as damaged goods. No one believed I deserved a good man. Truth is, somewhere deep down inside, I didn't believe it either. Maybe desire and passion would come. I would be a fool to let a good man go, right? I was going to prove to everyone that good can come to me. That was the conversation I had with myself over and over.

We would attend each other churches and we were high on Jesus. He was a true worshipper, which was something that I was impressed with. On September 4, 2016, he proposed and I said yes. Everyone was ecstatic and I immediately became a representation of hope for people. I had been through so much two failed marriages and there I was getting another chance at love. I began to get caught up in the hype.

In total transparency, I had decided not to get married. There were some things that I wasn't at peace with and had reached out for advice. I was advised not to get married, but every time someone saw him, they would thank him for loving me. They would go on and on about me finally getting the love I deserved. When I expressed how I felt about that to my friends, they would fuss at me. The consensus was, I needed to marry him because he was a good man and treated me the best I've ever been treated. One of my friends even got in my face as if she would fight me if I walked away. Needless to say, I was in conflict. Do I follow my head or my heart? There were some things that just didn't sit right with me, so I knew what I had to do I decided to call off the engagement, but when I got there, I choked. The fact that I would be responsible for hurting someone got the best of me, so I sucked up my feelings and rationalized all the reasons the marriage would work. It didn't help that the weddings plans were immaculate. Everything was going to be so beautiful and people were coming in from everywhere. Everyone was so happy, so who was I to disappoint the people?

On August 19, 2017, I got married. It was such a beautiful ceremony we had church. We praised God, the decor was out of this world and everyone looked so beautiful, especially me. We had a very festive reception, and we danced the night away. The next day we went to worship we had to give God the glory. That Sunday afternoon we had dinner with my family from Jacksonville and saw them off and the next day we headed out for our honeymoon.

After a week of celebrating, we returned home and that is when it hit me. I was married! What!? I began to have that rationalizing conversation with myself again. I even said, "I showed them. People counted me out but look at God". Isn't that what we do? We accredit something to God when it's of our own doing.

I did what I normally did, I smiled. Everyone would ask, "How is married life?" I would lie and say "great." Truth is, home was peaceful, God dwelled there, and the type of chaos I was used to no longer existed. Why was I complaining just because I wasn't happy? I had been told several times that God cares nothing about us being happy. I totally disagree with that now; however, at the time it was one of my indoctrinated beliefs, so I accepted it as a fact that I would never be happy.

I threw myself into ministry and as I was trying to get some new ministries going I was getting push back. God was giving me more vision, but I couldn't get certain things done without the approval of leadership. I just wanted to serve people. I was discouraged and church had become a miserable place for me. I started to become a hit and miss church member. When I did come, it was just to see my friends and then the next thing I knew, I had missed 7 straight weeks. What was sad about that was the leadership didn't reach out. When I was directing the choir and people were getting the benefit of my gift, everyone was shouting Hosanna! When I decided to step away to take care of my mental health and do ministry I was passionate about, it was like "crucify her." Before long I had stopped attending altogether. I became a faithful member of Bedside

Baptist. In addition to my strained relationship with church, I wasn't being fulfilled in my marriage and before I knew it, I was spiraling into a deep depression.

December 10, 2017 is a day I will never forget. It was the first time in a long time I felt suicidal. I just couldn't get my thoughts under subjection. I was crying and hollering for God to come rescue me. My husband started anointing the room and speaking over my life. I was having a full blown panic attack and I couldn't catch my breath. He rebuked the devil, laid his hands on me and called on the name of the Lord. After about two hours of that, I started to calm down and when I could finally speak, I told my husband that I had to get to somebody's church that day.

We ended up at New Jerusalem Cathedral and when I stepped out the car, I froze. I hadn't been to a church building in a minute. I started walking toward the building then I'd stop. My husband kept encouraging me to walk in. When I made it through the doors, I was greeted with so much love. Greeters were on both sides and one by one they welcomed me. One of the greeters knew my husband and said to me, "You are so beautiful." I've been looking forward to meeting you." Her hug was so warm and I immediately felt God. As we walked in, each usher had a smile and said "welcome". I couldn't believe how nice the people were. We got to the usher in the front and she escorted us to our seats. She asked if it was my first time there and when I responded with "Yes ma'am," she said "I will be standing in this area. If you need anything, let me know."

As she began to walk off, she turned around and said, "You are so beautiful. Would you mind if I take your picture after church?" Even though I thought it was a strange request, I thanked her and agreed. I looked at my husband and said, "God is here." The lady that did the call to worship was amazing. When she began to read the scripture that God placed in her heart, tears rolled down my face, I couldn't believe it. The scripture was Romans 8:18 my favorite scripture. "For I reckon that the sufferings of this present time are not worthy to be compared with the glory which shall be revealed in us." How could she know? She couldn't know. I looked at my husband again and said, "God is here." The praise team sang about God's promises. Every word was tailormade for me and I was bawling. The burden I came in with was lifted. When they asked first-time visitors to stand, I proudly stood. The choir sang a welcome song to us and I was in awe of God. When the pastor and his armor bearers entered, I sensed a readiness for the word. In his introduction, he said everything I needed to hear. It was like he had been in our house that morning. How could he know that I was fighting to stay alive just a few hours earlier? It felt like God had whispered in everyone's ear to save me. I worshipped without restraint for the first time in my life. I surrendered to God like never before and after service, the parishioners around me invited me to come back. I was about to walk out when the usher who wanted to take my picture stopped me. She said, "I'll take that picture now." They had a beautifully decorated Christmas tree on the stage, so I went up there to get my picture taken. She said, "Where is your phone?" I was confused but I gave her my phone. She took the picture, gave me back my phone, said "You're beautiful," and walked away. I immediately began to cry. It dawned on me that the picture was not for her, it was for me. God wanted me to see in spite of everything I had been through, I was beautiful. That day I felt a huge weight lifted.

I went back to church that night. Everybody acquainted with me at that time knew I didn't believe in no night church, but that day, I wanted more of Him. We attended practically every service and bible study and joined the church on December 31, 2017 and up until the global pandemic, that was where I worshipped.

I didn't realize how much I had covered and pretended until the world stopped. I couldn't hide behind church. I lost my job on May 29, 2020, the day my husband and I were going to see a house to purchase. I got fired two hours before that appointment. I couldn't believe it then, but now I understand. I couldn't get into a 30year commitment with my husband when we were hanging on by a thread. We were strangers living in the same space. We didn't have to pretend anymore. There were no more in person church services and there was no more meeting up with friends. We finally had to face the music. We had been struggling since day one and we had made decisions that were unbiblical and unconventional. We made choices that we knew would put the nail in our coffins and although we tried, we were at the point of no return.

What made matters more complicated is, towards the end of our marriage, I had fallen in love with someone else. As a Christian couple, we had opened some doors that should have remained closed. I will be the first to admit I was wrong. I wouldn't recommend anyone starting another relationship without ending the one you're in. I don't agree with the way I handle things; however, I was thankful that my husband and I agreed "we" ended a long time ago. When I left, we were both relieved. We loved each other enough to let each other go. Our divorce was the most amicable divorce I ever witnessed. As a matter of fact, the last day I saw him, we prayed together and wished each other the best in our new lives. In that moment, I didn't have to ask God what love was, I was experiencing it. Love sometimes means letting go we both breathed.

CHAPTER 9

"Love Finally Found Me"

To say that I am proud of myself is an understatement. I had accomplished something I had never done before. I chose me! For once I didn't care if anyone approved. I didn't ask for permission to do what was best for me. I didn't care how crazy I looked because I wasn't in search of anyone's acceptance or understanding. I was no longer a slave to outside validation. It was time for me to become my priority. I had been suffocating under my own pretense. I came to the conclusion I didn't have to lie anymore because my truth was enough. I made a decision to stop participating in my own suffering and I didn't want to just be free, I wanted to be delivered. I was a master at staying in familiar bondage and I was tired of dysfunctional comfort. I was no longer willing to stay in something just to please people. Life is too short. My ex-husband and I agreed that just because we are two good people didn't mean we were a good couple.

I had allowed the rules of religion to destroy my authentic relationship with Jesus. It dawned on me that I was in anguish because I had been loyal to a brook that never had water. In my transition of pursuing a quench for my thirst, God reminded me of the Samaritan woman at the well. Just like her, I had been at my well drawing and digging for water that could not fulfill me. I too had multiple marriages and the one I was with was not mine. I know what it's like to be dirty and to be considered filthy. I wondered if God could clean me up.

I am extremely grateful that in spite of my reputation, God gave me living water so that I would never have to thirst again and just like that Samaritan woman, in my excitement, I dropped my jar and ran to my community shouting "come see a man." It says in John 4:39 "because of her testimony, many Samaritans from the city believed on Him." I was hoping for the same results.

Unlike the Samaritan woman, however, I had to walk in edifices of worship where people would rather condemn my wounds than celebrate my scars. I was proud of my scars because they were evidence of survival. I've walked in communities of believers where my testimony was not wanted. "Tonya, you are too transparent with your life." I've met with leadership about needing a woman counselor on staff in hopes that more women would be comfortable sharing their stories of abuse and start their healing. I've suggested ministries like divorce care and grief care just to hear, "Tonya, we know these ministries are needed but we don't have money in the budget." I've been requested to speak on programs to empower women who had been victims of sexual abuse and domestic violence, but the leadership didn't want me there. I had ministers get in their pulpits and demand their congregations not to come to my empowerment conference. I know what it is like for leading women to want my influence, but not want me. "Tonya, can you give me so and so's phone number I need to contact her to see if she can speak at our ladies' day function." This is what I'm sure Jesus meant when he said, "a prophet is honored everywhere except in his own hometown and among his own family." I know what it is like to debate with the Jews, I mean Christians, about which temple is the true place of worship. It's funny to me that the same people who had so much to say about where I had chosen to worship were the same people who were silent when they could have helped me. Crazy how people can watch you suffer, but once you're safe and out of their toxic environment, they tell you God doesn't dwell where you worship. Where was the God in them when I needed them?

In the midst of all the rejection, I had been in turmoil about dissolving my marriage. The only person I could lean on was God. He was the only one up with me the nights I couldn't sleep. He was the only one who saw my tears, even when I was smiling. I didn't like who I was in the marriage, but I loved who I was in ministry, but ministry was not sustaining me. I was dying and I needed God to save me. I communicated with God fervently and we had so many deep conversations. I asked him if I was capable of love. I sought Him and He showed me what love was. I asked Him how it should feel, and I shared with Him what I wanted.

One day in all my confusion, I began watching an episode of "Black Love" on the OWN network. The episode was about this one couple who had gone through the devastating loss of their child. As I watched, I began to cry with and for them. I listened to their love story. I watched their body language. I could feel their love, connection, and devotion. I pointed to the television with tears in my eyes and I said out loud "God, I want to experience that." Three days later, (if you are a Christian, you know why I am about to shout as I write this) Caryl called me and expressed his feelings for me. He shared everything I had been feeling but was too afraid to share. As he was sharing, I looked towards heaven and told God "thank you." I had never known a love like this. If you felt connection before, you know what I am talking about. Life started to make sense. I was laughing again, I felt like dancing, and my heart was beating again. I had no desire for anyone or anything else. I was joyous and giddy like a schoolgirl. I knew this was it and I knew God had answered my prayer.

The reason I knew He was the one is because of the promise and pact I had made with myself. I promised myself if I was to ever fall in love, the man's love for me had to feel like it exceeded the love I had for myself. I love me some Tonya. Caryl was determined to outdo me, and he still does. We are soulmates and before him, I didn't even believe that was a true thing. He is my best friend. He even shared his feelings with my parents, telling them they didn't have to worry about me anymore; he would protect me at all cost. He told them I was safe, and I shared with him all the gross details of my life and he still wanted to love me. He even said any cross I was carrying he would now carry because it was my time to rest. He even quoted that line from Tyler's Perry movie "Diary of a Mad Black Woman." He said, "Tonya, all you have to do is wake up and I'll take it from there." He has kept every word of his promise.

As I was completing this book, I worried about how people close to him would view me. I struggled with the thought of someone questioning him on how he could love someone like me. He assured me that we would remain. He promised to love me longer than forever and I love who I am with him. Because of my relationship with him, I was introduced to myself. No one can come between this love. God has answered my prayer and I will never take his love for granted. I am so happy.

Whenever you decide to choose yourself, the people who benefitted from your misery fall off. I believe if people love you, they would be happy because you're happy. I am a firm believer that you can love someone and not agree with them. I will admit that I was hurt to my core when my close friends walked away. It showed me the sisterhood I valued was not reciprocated. I found out the hard way that people will walk away if they don't approve of your choice. I had to accept that their season in my life was up. I refused to keep feeding people while they were starving me. I had to let go and accept their gift of goodbye.

My peace is knowing what man demands, God never required. I was God's anointed and I belonged to Him. I found comfort in knowing God loves me even when Christians don't. I am convinced that some people believe if they dissociate themselves from you, God does too. False. Truth is, God and I are closer than we've ever been. The love that I finally found was HIM. Before I made any moves, I talked to God. People assume if you don't live by their playbook, you are outside of the will of God, but my safety was never in the church, but in God. The church molested, raped, used, rejected, betrayed, bullied, and wounded me, but it did not damage or kill me. Ironically, God used all of that stuff to birth me. I finally found love because I was becoming the Tonya He created me to be.

I've been asked how I could continue to attend church. People wonder how I can continue to minister to people who don't like me. My response is this: It is not about me. I minister because God gave me the assignment and I must be about my father's business. I am very clear that my story is not about me. It's for others to witness the goodness of God. My testimony is going to increase someone else's faith. God will get the glory from my life. I want to be a billboard of hope and I believe that there is nothing you can't overcome.

Yes, I was wounded in worship, but God restored me and because He did, I am now free to worship. I have learned that whatever God allowed was for my good God is sovereign! I am thankful for my valleys because they were the pathways to my mountain top. God had counted and collected each one of my tears. He knew what it would take for me to become. No more shame no more guilt no more looking back. I have exchanged my pain for purpose.

I sing with gladness:

When peace like a river attendeth my way,

When sorrow like sea billows roll;

Whatever my lot, Thou has taught me to say,

It is well, it is well with my soul.

Until we meet again, I encourage you to live your life unfiltered, unashamed, and unapologetically. Don't carry a cross of past failures. Don't be afraid of doing whatever God has placed in your hands to do.

It is also my prayer that we give each other grace because you never know what a person has gone through. Some stuff people are carrying is heavy, so I pray that instead of judging behavior, we will love enough to meet the need to help heal each other's pain.

Just because you're wounded doesn't mean you're damaged. God specializes in restoring what's broken. God is Jehovah Rapha and in Him, you can find rest for your soul.

THE ACTUAL WORDS IN THE LETTER I SENT TO THE PREACHER WHO TOOK MY VIRGINITY

July 13, 2010

It is my prayer that this letter finds you and your family well.

Amazingly, 22 years after my first encounter with you , I found myself not being able to move forward, but however allowed my unfortunate experience with you to bind me physically, emotionally, mentally, and most importantly, spiritually. Losing my virginity to you has scared me like no other experience in my life. As a young adult, I trusted the God in you to be my mentor, my protector and leader. I also relied on you because you were a gospel preacher and my father's friend. Little did I know that my life would be shaped and molded by my affair with you. At the time, I was naïve and wanted to please you. I remember just like it was yesterday. The first time your tried to sleep with me, I rejected you and you didn't speak to me for two days. You treated me so evil, so I remember faking a fainting spell on stage because I knew you wouldn't have a choice but to come see about me. That night, I would lose my virginity. I remember when it was over, you looked down and saw the blood and said, "You wasn't lying." You were a virgin." I remember getting dressed and you dropping me off at the home that I would sleep for the night. I couldn't believe what just happened. I couldn't sleep. I swam in the pool most of the night trying to clear my head. This begins another mask with my Lord and my friends. Summer '88. From there my affair with you would last through my sophomore year. Through me being an honor student. Through me being crowned Miss Southwestern. And I got back together in my sophomore year. I remember you giving him work study job in your office so people wouldn't think it strange that I would be at your office. Oh the facade I had to live. On one hand I was this great student and leader. On the other hand, I was the chief of sinners. Those worlds would come to a head when I tried to commit suicide at school. And others would come to my rescue. would make me walk the track all night because I just wanted to sleep. He could not let me fall to sleep or I would die. When he knew I was safe, he took me to my room. You of course came to my room the next morning. News had traveled fast. You told me what to tell Bro. (lie), so I wouldn't get kicked out of school. I did and said exactly what you told me to say and do. At this time, I'm so deeply in love so I thought. Until that fateful night, you called me at my dorm and told me you would never leave your wife and instructed me how to take care of myself sexually. Wow still letting you be in control.

Thank God for graduation day. I remember feeling sad because I would miss my friends but feeling relieved that the charade would be over. Little did I know, you being my father's friend gave you continued access to me.

Well, needless to say, I did exactly what everyone thought I would do, I acted like nothing happened and this affair didn't bother me or my life to come. Oh how wrong I was. I began to do things with men that I thought I'd never do. Started to drown out this experience by drinking. I would do anything to understand if God wasn't good enough for a gospel preacher, how would He be good enough for me? God couldn't love me. Why would He let me get caught up? Why would I only feel good when I was lying on my back? To make matters worse, I slept with you again when you were speaking in High Point.

Yes, I remember the day at the National Lectureship that you apologized because you were the adult and I was the child. I did what I often do, I said "It's ok, Bro. ". 'Tm fine." However, I wasn't. My thoughts were about protecting you. I didn't want my father to be mad at me. "Tonya, you'll be okay," is what I told myself. There were times through the years that I was able to hear you preach. I was able to come sing at your congregation. Then one day out of the blue, I was told you'll be preaching at Southside. You see, by this time my father is full aware not only of the affair but how damaging it was for me. I couldn't understand it. I told my husband, I would be okay. Little did I know that when I saw you walking behind my father heading to the pulpit, my heart would sink. I couldn't breathe. I had to walk out. I went home and cried all night. I remember wanting to die. How could my father bring you here? What kind of loyalty is this?

Well, needless to say, after I finished expressing myself to my father, I hadn't had to experience you preaching to an audience at

Southside that I was in. However, he just recently came to your place. You've been to golf tournaments. I still can't figure it out.

Well, the good news is that I finally understand. God does love me! What the devil meant for bad, God has worked it out for my good. God has given me the ability to use all my pain, hurt, disappointment and failures to help others. I am an outstanding speaker, teacher, writer, performer, and encourager. I am the most compassionate woman I know. I have a heart for the hurting. I know God and experience God's redemption and transformation every day. I now have an annual women's conference entitled "I Was Not Built to Break." God is using me in a powerful way. I give Him all the Glory. He chose me! I guess you are wondering why it was important for me to contact you now. You were the piece I couldn't get past. I know you and my father talked about it. I didn't know what I did to deserve this. I thought it was unfair that you were able to go on with your life achieving this or that and I was stuck with hatred, bitterness, and resentment. You had to know as a doctor who deals with the mind and behavior, there is no way I could be fine after such an experience. You know that I would be scarred and would need help to navigate through such pain. Well, I did go to therapy. Even though it was intense, revealing, and hard, I am free. I no longer have to be angry. I don't have to let this experience dictate who I am anymore. God has renewed my heart, mind, and my soul. I no longer have a hole in my soul. My service is motivated not so much by the hurt but by the change in my life. People love me for my transparency and authenticity. There are so many women who have been hurt by preachers, fathers, men in the church and I am the lady God is using to help heal their brokenness. God is so AMAZING! So, Philippians 1:6 is true, "being confident of this, that He who began a good work in you will carry it on to completion until the day of Christ Jesus.

I forgive you and I forgive me. MOVING FORWARD!!!! I BREATHE!

Please know that I don't want anything from you. As a doctor, you are aware it is so beneficial for the damaged party to be able to release their feelings to move forward. Don't need a response, contact or apology. What God has for you is for you.

LaTonya

(Names removed from the letter to protect the innocent

The Masked Pulpiteer

Your position is one anointed to comfort and heal;
Yet you decided to use it to destroy, kill and steal.

Stole a young lady's innocence while portraying this "holy" grace;
A devastating event where her freedom was taken and displaced.

Her new walk exposes a disposition of guilt and shame;
An anger unspeakable because she feels that God's the blame.

The word says, "How can they hear unless a preacher is sent?
So how could you make the god news a message of damnable contempt?

You didn't care that you left a catastrophic wound crippling her for life;
You just moved on and made her live with the bitterness and strife.

You still were able to teach Gods Word…seeking and saving the lost;
Yet you let her a saint in sin for others to crucify on YOUR cross.

You didn't lose anything for your family and friends remained;
Yet she suffered and was stagnated for her heart was
permanently stained.

You turned Gods' love into a myth and preyed on her soul;
BEWARE for you'll reap what you sowed when you're rejected from
"The Streets Paved with Gold."

Well, in time she saw behind your mask and realized God loved her still;
Now her pain is purpose showing others how great redemption feels!

Lord, Help Me Through My Devastating Storm"

Lord, please give me the strength to hang in there;
All I feel is hopelessness and uncontrollable despair.

I know you wouldn't suffer me with more than I can bear;
But if I'm not mistaken I'm way pass there.

The road I'm traveling is full of sadness and pain.
I know you're purging me, yet I feel from this trial there's nothing for me to gain.

I can't begin to put a smile on my face;
My laughter dissolved by tears and my soul has no place.

I feel life has dealt me a rotten and unfair hand;
But I only have myself to blame because I didn't stay in Your plan.

I feel so low and that I just can't go on;
It's like my life is beyond repair and permanently torn.

I try to lift my head but it's so heavy with sorrow;
I often feel that I don't want to see tomorrow.

Even though I'm down and feel this way;
I'm sure You're saying, "have faith, You know I promised a brighter day."

I try to rest on Your Blessed Assurance and Grace;
Because I plan to make it home in spite of this difficult race.

I want so much for You to move this mountain out of my way;
Yet, I will hold on because You're just a prayer away.

Lord, there is no other help I know so I reach out my hand to You;
I know regardless of this wretched pain You'll see me through.

Lord, I ask You that I allow my faith to blossom as a rose.
When this trial has passed I know I made it over because it was peace in You I chose.

LaTonya Renae ©2011

"The Fallen Child's Prayer"

God with Your loving eyes look deep into my heart;
Rescue me from myself o we won't remain apart.

There was a time You could always count on me.
Yet, my own lust and temptation blinded me and I couldn't see.

Oh dear God, what has happened to Your child?
My life so tangled that I've forgotten how to bow.

Oh, God, if only I could turn back the hands of time
when I was so faithful.
But in a blink of an eye, I've become so selfish and ungrateful.

Father, renew my strength and faith in Thy word.
May I realize my soul being lost is something I can't afford.

As I call out to You, please anoint me now;
Reign down on me and lead Your Spirit to endow.

May I return to You for You have never failed;
For I want to be a vessel that Redemption upheld.

This world has nothing to offer me;
For only through Your love will I ever be free.

Opened arms always providing mercy and grace;
Running back to You is surety that I'll run a successful race.

And when I reach eternity and
And shout around Your precious throne;
Oh, how glad I will be that my soul will be home.

Now, God, watch over me as I dwell in this world
and live by Your plan;

That when I expire from this life,
I'll shout I made it because I held on to the Master's hand.

Tonya, I Apologize

Father, my Creator

I thank You for allowing my eyes to be open physically and spiritually.

It amazes me the wondrous works of Thy hands. I see You in the rain, the sun, the birds, the swaying trees, Your people, my inhaling, and exhaling. And today I especially see You in my smile. Of course You know I speak of the smile in my heart, it's not heavy today. The amazing thing is my situation hasn't changed however my attitude towards my situation has changed. I see You building my character and strength as You strip away those people and things I called security. Intellectually I've always known there's nobody greater than You. Your love has given me the fortitude to remain safe in You and the desire to live out my testimony. I apologize to You for not taking care of my soul, spirit, mind, and body. You have given me stewardship over myself and I have failed You. And now I'm running back to You.

Tonya,

My sweet inner soul, I apologize to you. You desire so much to be a vessel of honor. You love God with all you have. Through your pain, trials, purpose, and triumphs, you just want to live for Him. I'm sorry that I've often led you astray. In my search for love I handed my heart to those who were also wounded, broken and in search for love themselves. We all so desperately want to be love. I have made you suffer because of my lack of wisdom and craving of my flesh. I looked for validation in people and what I thought their love could give me. I apologize for taking you down in the pits of hell.

Tonya,

My gentle spirit, I apologize to you for ignoring your desperate attempts to save me. Often I could hear you and feel you but I did what my flesh desired. You sent warning after warning but I chose not to listen. Now I know there's a big difference between affection

and love. I now know tears from loneliness are sweeter than tears of heartbreak. I apologize for grieving you.

Tonya,

My tender mind, I apologize for exposing you with thoughts that produced damaging behavior. I filled you with self-doubt, anger, bitterness, revenge, and worthlessness. Most of my life I turned you over to others to lead you. I didn't give you a voice. For this I apologize.

Tonya,

My precious body, oh how I have violated you. I apologize for abusing you and for allowing others to abuse you. From an early age I was taught that my body was the temple of God. I've often wished I would have valued you more. For all the destruction I caused you, I apologize.

Tonya,

Today as you begin again, may you forgive yourself for not seeing what was right in front of you the entire time. And that is you are a masterpiece. You are still here in spite of all the devil has thrown at you. You are not your mistakes. You are not defined by your past. You will not be afraid to love. In time God will send someone to love you. Remember you are not anyone else's mistakes. You can't any longer be the scapegoat for anyone else's failures. Stop blaming yourself for people's weaknesses and lies. You are better than that. You can't fix people. You can't even fix yourself. God is the only healer. You have a lot to offer yourself and the world. Don't be afraid to step out and enjoy yourself. God told you to live. Don't let human love continue to kill you. Stand firm in God's love. For His love is eternal.

What happens when your wounds are produced at the cross? What do you do when the place of light is the darkest place on earth? What a journey it's been to see the manifestation of the devil's desire to "sift me as wheat." How many times have I reached out to "touch the hem of Jesus' garment" just to be stepped on by His leaders? Can you imagine being left in so many pieces? You have a feeling of hopelessness and wonder if you could ever become whole. BUT GOD!!! The good news is when wounds heal they turn into scars. Scars are evidence that what was meant to destroy you, you SURVIVED it! To God be the GLORY!!!

Author LaTonya Renae Smith is an Empowerment Enthusiast! She is a Certified Life Coach and Founder/CEO of Tonya'z Embrace, LLC. In addition to being the hostess of "I Was Not Built to Break' Empowerment Conference, LaTonya is also the hostess of "Transparent Thursdays."

As a motivational speaker, she is known as the "Voice for the Voiceless" and believes you can OVERCOME

Made in the USA
Columbia, SC
10 May 2025

57764500R00080